MW01488181

Has America Lost Her Way?

By
Robert E. Williams

PublishAmerica
Baltimore

© 2004 by Robert E. Williams.
All rights reserved. No part of this book may be reproduced, stored in a retrieval system or transmitted in any form or by any means without the prior written permission of the publishers, except by a reviewer who may quote brief passages in a review to be printed in a newspaper, magazine or journal.

First printing

ISBN: 1-4137-4235-1
PUBLISHED BY PUBLISHAMERICA, LLLP
www.publishamerica.com
Baltimore
Printed in the United States of America

To Tony

from your Bob
uncle
8/26/06

Robert E. William

For my children, their children,
and *your* children.

*May this book recommend
a love of God and Country.*

ACKNOWLEDGMENTS

Wife, Peggy, deserves to be decorated for the trips, and for dinners-out she has missed the last few years, and for the long-promised clean garage that is still a hazard to life and limb. Generous with her time, and always there, she patiently proofed each page as I made my repeated changes of living history as it occurred.

Dozens of friends call my attention to world events which support my vision of world history, contribute books, and insights which are always welcomed. Daughter, Patricia and her husband Phil Kaster, showed me some intricacies of Microsoft Word and Publisher, which seem to slip away in the fog as soon as they left, as though the computer listened only to them. It is amazing that I could be a student of computers for twenty years, and learn something new every day.

And a very special thanks to my good friend of many years, Ernest Grizzard, whose technical assistance in putting the book together helped smooth the transition from draft files to completed book on compact disk.

The encouragement to write the book came from Clare-Parris Wyrick from Savannah, who writes a Letter to the Editor almost every week for the *Savannah News*, debating with the area Liberals. She said this book should have been published ten years ago, when I first started writing it, and be required reading in every university in America. Current events seem to support her recommendation.

FOREWORD

The conflict between Islam and Christianity is the problem of our time. It swamps all other problems. On the outcome of this struggle depends the future of all mankind.

This conflict first revealed itself as a war between Communism and Freedom in the 1950s. It appears to some that Communism is dead and Freedom has won. Not true. The war is simmering like a hot bed of coals just under the surface of the culture. Islam has joined the fight.

Communism, Islam and Socialism are brothers under the skin. All three live under dictatorships, with ambitions to rule the world, and vow the ultimate murder of all who resist. All three vow that capitalism, the system of government that has given mankind the only freedom it has ever known, must go.

The war started as a communist revolution in America in 1936, picked up and spread like wildfire by indoctrinated liberal intellectuals, and communist indoctrinated professors in school. They taught you to hate America, to hate our form of government, and to hate our president.

This is not the story you learned in school, nor is it the story being taught to your children today. You learned that it was Capitalist, Imperialist, War Monger America who butted into civil wars in both Korea and Vietnam.

The truth is, America, observing that the communists were gobbling up nations like popcorn and controlled a third of the world, over 900 million people, drew lines in the sand and announced to the communist world, "you are not going to take another country."

When Communism withdrew into its strategic retreat, Islam was standing ready to step into its shoes, to advance its own agenda for world domination.

True to form, moles are saying "welcome to our world" to millions of Muslims, who are swamping our nation while cheering on the Terrorists.

TABLE OF CONTENTS

OVERVIEW

One puzzles at how the character of the American public could have changed so much in one generation. In less than 20 years we went from a unified nation of heroes during World War II to a splintered nation, where millions would riot in the streets, calling for their country to unilaterally surrender, and lay down its arms in the face of an enemy sworn to its destruction.

Further, the rioters would take unto themselves a mantle of idealism, and a loathing for capitalism, a system that has given mankind the only freedom it has ever known. The society they favored promises a higher freedom, but delivers slavery and butchery on a scale unprecedented in the history of man, and an economic order which offers its followers no more than a bare existence.

The Idealism of the 60s Misplaced

The students' idealism envisioned the destruction of the materialistic status quo practiced by their parents in America, in favor of a culture where there is no private property, which they were taught is the root of all evil. They became cynics, indoctrinated to believe that:

- Religion is a capitalist idea to keep the populace under control.
- Marriage is a capitalist idea for men to keep women as private property.
- Property rights are to keep wealth in the hands of a few when it really belongs to all the people, managed by a central government.
- Children do not really belong to the parents who birthed them, but rather to all the people, to the society of which they are but a fragment.
- The results of the labor of those who can work should go into a public storehouse, to be withdrawn by all according to their needs.
- With no private property there would be no need for a police force, no need for government, no moral judgments, no religious problems, no problems with money, markets and prices, and no crime.

15

This is a bit of the utopia promised to our children. It was a communist utopia which would supposedly come to pass after the capitalist society of America was destroyed.

Hundreds of thousands bought into it.

A Communist Under Every Bed

This revolution was not going unnoticed. In the early 1950s, there arose in America what many liberals have proclaimed as the darkest period in our history, when neurotics were finding a communist under every bed, and everything that went wrong was a communist plot.

It seemed that a huge part of our population had suddenly gone mad, and started accusing everybody in sight. Some now say that one-out-of-ten Americans may have fallen under the communist spell, but that is unlikely. The communists didn't need numbers to create chaos. They wanted the energy and idealism of the youth of America, the minds of the intellectuals, along with infiltrators and agitators in critical positions throughout the society and government. The numbers would come through indoctrination and agitation.

The Cold War Began in 1936

History records that as World War II wound down, the Soviet Union resumed its policy of "gathering nations," of which America and capitalism was primary on their list.

The war against capitalism was initially declared in 1936, but while it had early successes, wasn't making much progress.

Americans interested in the utopia they promised, often viewed it though democratic eyes. They didn't see themselves as serfs, with chains to be cast off, but as free men and women, who preferred to fight any revolution through the democratic process. They really didn't know what to make of the crazy Soviets and weren't so warm to the idea of the "dictatorship of the proletariat."

In the 50s and 60s American students and intellectuals, by and large, were probably not interested in becoming a part of the Soviet Union but were susceptible to the communist propaganda which pointed out America's problems and the communist Utopia n solution.

Soviet Union Makes Tactical Change

At the end of WWII the Soviets re-declared their war and changed their tactics. They knew breaking the will of America would take some time, and so announced four five-year plans. First they would take Europe, then Africa, then Asia, and by what figured to be about 1973 America would "fall into our hands like a ripe plum." Keep that date, 1973, in your mind.

Actually the kind of threat they presented was advanced to the 13 colonies back in 1776 by Thomas Paine when he wrote, *"...some dictator may hereafter arise, who laying hold of popular disquietudes, collect together the desperate and discontented, and by assuming themselves the power of government, sweep away the liberties of a continent like a deluge. Ere we could hear the news, the fatal business might be done, and ourselves left suffering under the oppression of a conqueror."*

This was the plan the Soviet Union had for America and other countries on their list. They would even help with uncovering disquietudes if you couldn't think of any.

The Soviet Plan For America

The Soviet plan, in addition to being a strong military threat, involved a simple system of infiltration, agitation and propaganda. A few undercover agents who spoke the language fluently, would go into a targeted country, find out what the public was most concerned about, stir up people on both sides of the controversy, and keep stirring the problem until the argument got out of hand.

In the meantime they would infiltrate and neutralize all parts of the society, universities, schools, church, government, family, anywhere they might expect resistance.

The result they were after was a public, confused, frightened, not sure what to believe, no longer sure about their country, their religion, or their culture.

The process used a technique called in some circles, "brainwashing" and so captured the attitudes and behavior of the public that it effectively neutralized the American legal system where communism was concerned. Much as the military would take out air defenses, they took out the legal defenses. Instead of saturation bombing they saturated us with lies and propaganda.

The infiltration process included all levels of the government including the Office of the President, and major universities, most notably law and journalism schools. It used the media and rock music to spread its propaganda, resulting in widespread deterioration of American moral values, and of traditional American patriotism.

The psychological warfare was simple as we shall show, involving a process called "informing" and "self criticism" to divide America into warring factions, and then pouring an idealistic education into the resulting emotional vacuum.

It was deceitful in that the propaganda they used was not identified as being communist. So clever was the deceit that many whose minds were captured will swear to this day, no communists were involved. What they were doing was sold to them by Americans as being in the highest traditions of American morality and liberty.

The communists used the same brainwashing system to gain and keep control in every communist country on earth.

A Great Way To Run A War

It is a great way to run a war. All the infrastructure remains in good shape; the buildings, highways, and airports are intact; only a few "hopeless reactionaries" who insist upon defending their country are killed, including no Russians. In this manner they toppled country after country.

The American public began to notice that, with this system, and little other duress, they had taken over Europe and a great deal of Africa and had their sights set on Korea and Cuba. They controlled a third of the world - over 900 million people.

America looked on in what has been called the Cold War, and while the discussion as to what action to take was hot and heavy, all we could agree upon was, it was better than shooting.

The Public Began To Take Notice

Then we began to notice that the communists had infiltrated America like termites in an old barn. Soviet agents were found in all levels and departments of our government including the Office of The President.

Since it was a crime to be a communist in the early days, many were identified and sent to jail. Communists began to turn states-evidence, identifying other communists to lighten their own sentences.

There was a limited number of people they could send over here without being noticed, so the revolution in many, maybe most, cases was being handled by indoctrinated Americans, with only one or two communist agents in each group or cell.

The dupes and fellow travelers were taught to hate capitalism, and were sympathetic with what the communists were doing. Feeling that great changes needed to be made in America, they would take on any ally.

Media and Movie Makers Get Into The Act

Recruited and indoctrinated movie makers began making films with social messages against the status quo. Any kind of authority figure - preacher, father, military officer, policeman, teacher, government leader, including the President - began to be presented as idiots and fools, with all the good graces residing in kids, women, minorities, homosexuals, underdogs and even the family dog.

Dad and the cop on the corner were ignorant pigs. Religion and patriotism was for nerds and honoring something like a flag was, well, laughable. As they gained more confidence, films featuring drugs, drunks, weirdos, and anti-establishment themes became the norm. This continues to this day and is getting even worse.

What the movie makers started presenting in 1948 is in stark contrast to the movies they displaced - westerns, musicals, family sitcoms, and military films glorifying freedom and American patriotism.

Madness in America

William Murchison, *The Dallas Morning News* columnist, said in a recent column that "..., it becomes harder to recall that not long ago American culture didn't think that the sexes are practically interchangeable, didn't think that white males are good for nothing but oppressing others, didn't think of Western civilization as evil. Common sense, broadly speaking, ruled."

He reported that Martin L. Gross wrote in his new book, *The End of Sanity: Social and Cultural Madness in America* that "journalists, college administrators, bureaucrats, clergy, judges, artists, etc., seek to remake American culture in its own image. That image is pro-feminist, pro-racial preferences, pro-unchecked immigration, anti-Western civilization."

"'The country is going crazy' is the curt, angry phrase heard everywhere. On every societal front nonsense is replacing good sense in our once pragmatic nation," Murchison wrote. One can be sure the revolutionists, who are still around, are watching this "disquietude" with great interest in it becoming a major conflict.

Legal Vultures Move In

Indoctrinated lawyers, lawyers in search of a buck, along with the ACLU, always eager to file a case that upset the status quo, began to file lawsuits on behalf of the communists. They have now succeeded in removing virtually every law that we had to combat the menace. Our law enforcement and the FBI are virtually neutralized and out of business insofar as communists are concerned. Some analysts say the Constitution as presently interpreted by the judiciary is no longer able to provide for the common defense against an adversary from within.

Communists were turned free and ordered returned to their old jobs. It was made legal to teach the overthrow of America through force and violence so long as they didn't carry guns. Burning the flag and rioting in the streets became freedom of speech.

Ethics in the Law

You may have seen the guided discussion recently on public television moderated by a Harvard law professor about ethics in the law. Supreme Court Justice Antonin Scalia, past Speaker of the House of Representatives Newt Gingrich, and a number of prominent judges and lawyers were part of the panel.

The strong message they left was, *there are no ethics in the law*. Judges are not there to seek truth and justice. They are merely umpires between lawyers who "must represent their clients, even if they know they are guilty," and present them as if they were not guilty. The truth is not required from a lawyer in court. You can go to jail for lying in court, but any lawyer can lie to you, about you, for you, or against you. He can lead or mislead. The court does not require the truth from lawyers.

Everyone is entitled to a lawyer even if he is a subversive. National security is not a consideration. The best performance in the opinion of the judge, or the jury as charged by the judge, wins. There is no longer any such thing as justice under the law. There is only the law. The law is what the most talented lawyers say it is.

My question is, should it be called a "legal profession" which implies ethics where there are none? We have all heard juries say, "We all knew he was guilty, but the prosecutor didn't do a good job of making their case." The only ethics is keeping quiet if they know their client is guilty.

Justice Scalia defended this system, saying that out of the conflict between the lawyers would hopefully come truth and justice. Was the judiciary like this before the so-called Cold War? I don't think so.

Professors Join the Lawyers

Liberal-minded professors in the ivy-league universities seemed particularly receptive to the promised utopia. Those who were convicted and sent to jail for being a member of the communist party, and/or for teaching the violent overthrow of the United States, or of giving aid and comfort, support, money, attending communist meetings, and holding fund-raising rallies - were released from jail and returned to their old positions, free to continue spouting their poison.

The People Join the Battle — Congress Intervenes

The Congress, not blind to what was happening, through the House Un-American Activities Committee and Senate committees began to shine a light on communists wherever they could be found. They couldn't throw a communist in jail anymore but they could expose them.

They really hit pay dirt in Hollywood, with at least 280 actors, actresses, writers, directors and producers blackballed by their studios, and ten sent to jail for a year for contempt of court.

Our children — under the influence of these pink professors and the pink media with their dreams of the "heaven on earth utopia" the communists had promised — dropped out, condemned their parents for their materialism, became hippies living in communes and campgrounds with drugs and free love available to all.

During the Vietnam war they hit the streets in huge numbers in support of an alien power engaged in killing other Americans, cheered on by a horde of rock and roll bands with their bad grammar set to noise, praising peace and the drug culture. A leader in this pursuit was a British band called the Beatles, still revered by the 60s generation.

A million or more "peaceniks," including the President's daughter, gathered on the mall in Washington to demand America unilaterally ban the atomic bomb, while the Soviets kept theirs.

The Atomic Bomb Given to the Soviet Union

We now know that communist sympathizers in the Office of the President and the State Department actually gave our plans and the uranium for the atomic bomb to the Soviets along with the plans for the top secret Manhattan Atomic Energy Project.

Military police intercepted the first of several Soviet airplanes on the ground at the Lend-Lease base in Great Falls, Montana, late on the night of June 10, 1943, being loaded with suitcases full of Top Secret material, marked "from Hiss ." A call to Washington by the Soviet officer in charge of the shipment resulted in orders to the U.S. military police by Secretary of State Harry Hopkins, to release the Soviet aircraft and the plans, make no records and keep quiet about it.

War in America a Great Success

The war in America was so successful that now there is more stigma attached to anti-communists and Christianity than to communists and atheism. The communists didn't lose the Cold War or the Korean War or the Vietnam War. They won them all in the classrooms and on the streets of America. American students were misled and deceived. What the neo-Marxist professors were supporting and proclaiming was revolution all right, but at the expense of freedom as we know it. The political philosopher, Isaiah

Berlin, is quoted as saying, "…the higher freedom they proclaimed was equality in communism where in the end the individual's personal freedom is crushed underfoot and millions of heads roll."

History apparently has buried Marxism's ambitions, but there is evidence everywhere the ambitions are merely planted to spring up later. Marxist socialism is not dead. It is only out of sight for a time. It could be revived as early as the next election in Russia.

For America the Cold War had two distinct parts. There was the military threat with Soviets rattling their missiles and "gathering nations" and there was the political and psychological revolution taking place underground.

The military part of the Cold War can be said to be over, (not by me), but the political and psychological war is picking up steam.

Marxism is Not Dead

The students of the '60s in America are the leaders of today. Abraham Lincoln is quoted as saying, "The philosophy of the classrooms of one generation is the philosophy of government in the next." Our judges and lawyers, writers, politicians, and professors, are products of the period when ideas of a grand new world were taught. The philosophy of the classroom in the 60s was that capitalism as we know it, has to go.

What was past President Clinton thinking when he put the Russian president on the board of directors of NATO? Didn't we learn anything in the UN? Or does he have a different vision of how the world should be organized?

What is he thinking when he opens the White House to China, accepts money from them, and embraces the remaining remnant of the Evil Empire on this planet? The president chided the Chinese president that he was "not in step with history," suggesting that, he, Clinton, may believe in the *inevitability of history* learned as a member of the Radical Left. One gets the idea that the Chinese may have measured and assigned the offices in preparation for the revolution. They had free enough access. They may even have the keys to the building.

The fact is, we know more about China than we ever knew about Russia, having fought a war against them. You can read about the brainwashing of seven thousand Americans who were captured and lived for a time as unwilling guests in a Chinese Communist society in Appendix B. We know they called us, and still believe we are, a "paper tiger." We know China has murdered millions more of their own people than the Russians ever did.

What is this philosophy that seduced nearly half of the world and in spite of the fact it collapsed under its own weight and fell into bankruptcy, is still visibly threatening our freedoms and way of life. What is the control system they used to keep millions of people in bondage?

Direct Connection Exists Between the '50s and '60s and Today

Most Americans today are alarmed and concerned about America with its drugs and crime and permissiveness. Many say we are fast becoming a nation of barbarians and that there seems to be a direct correlation between what happened in the '50s and '60s, and what continues to this day.

The moral decay is piling up in our homes and streets and minds like garbage in our largest cities during a garbage workers' strike. Only, no one is taking any of it away and the stinking piles get bigger and bigger with no let-up in sight.

There is hope. Mr. Gross wrote that today's average American is "more stable, more sensible, and better-intentioned than our institutions" that seem unaware there is a problem and that they are it.

Murchison said that what we need are soap crews to undertake the huge task of cleansing our institutions. We must clean up and repair some of these flaws in our national character, so that history does not record the Fall of America, and what it once was like when men were free.

The Ball Is Passed to Islam

The present state of American culture gives "Open Sesame" to Islamic invaders with most of the preparatory work done for them. An invading Army numbering millions has slipped illegally across our borders, in just the past ten years. Why are they here, and why now in the wake of 9/11? Some say most of the Muslims recently entering this country, will make good freedom-loving, peace-loving

American citizens. When? Maybe, when they change our government, and all the Christians are dead? We allocate funds to feed, house, clothe and educate them, yet scarcely one Muslim anywhere in the world, to my knowledge, has publicly condemned the 9/11 terrorists. Their purpose here is transparent.

There are few, if any, laws remaining that America can use to defend itself against an internal enemy. The American Civil Liberties Union (ACLU) and the Supreme Court have removed all the stumps and stones in the road, and paved the path for our enemies. As this is written U.S. forces in Iraq have just captured the "Butcher of Bagdad," Saddam Hussein, who has murdered millions of his own citizens, and opened up the debate as to where to try him. It is clear that a trial in the United States, under present U. S. Law, with American lawyers and judges, would give him a better than even chance of escaping the death penalty. The best advice is try him anywhere but in America.

Our laws, originally passed or changed in the 60s and 70s, are skewed to the benefit of the guilty, and virtually useless where national defense is an issue. It is within the power of the Congress to clean them up, but no legislators seem to have the courage to take on the liberal courts.

A news story in the *Dallas Morning News* on March 7, 2003 revealed that the Berkner High School in Richardson near Dallas, allows the Muslim community to use its classrooms after hours to conduct religious services. They admit they teach the kids in American classrooms that infidels who don't believe in Islam, must ultimately be converted or killed. This, at a time when just the word "Christianity" cannot be uttered in any American school. Does Separation of Church and State apply to Muslims or is it just for Christianity? I watched for Letters to The Editor of protest. There were none. At least none were printed that I found. Who permitted this? It was the lawyers and the courts, and allowed to stand by a pliant Congress.

Are Liberals the Weapon of Mass Destruction?

Liberals in the State Department are reportedly impounding funds voted for the war against Terrorism, and releasing funds to outfit schools to train Arab fighters here and abroad. Liberal senators are stonewalling presidential nominees for vacant judicial positions who stand for defense of America, while demanding a litmus test for traitor.

The primary thread that connects the brains of these State Department liberal s, the liberal Democrat Senators, the offending Supreme Court judges, and ACLU lawyers is, they all seem to be blind to the defense of America, and open to its enemies. The Patriot Law enacted since 9/11, attempts to re-activate past laws against treason to combat terrorism, to an uproar of protest by Liberals.

Thomas Sowell writes that talk of a "living Constitution" conceals the fact that it is in fact dying, being re-interpreted out of existence, wherever it stands in the way of the evolving standards of socialist liberal think tanks. The trend to make law instead of interpret it, reportedly started with the Warren Court in the 50s. At the time there was a groundswell in America to impeach Earl Warren, Chief Justice of the Supreme Court. Nothing came of it and the trend is common practice.

Today, we can just about remove the word communism every place you see it here, and replace it with the words "militant Islam." The danger to freedom is not gone with the fall of communism. The ball has been passed to other hands. The Arab world is similar to the old Communist world in many ways. They are both Socialist with cruel dictatorship leaders. They share the goal that capitalism has to go, and of murdering the infidels.

American intellectuals appear comfortable with Muslims moving into church buildings left vacant when Christians moved out, and turning them into mosques. Thousands of new mosques are being built all over America, on land openly acquired for the purpose, private buildings with no general public access. In other countries mosques are arsenals, armed to the teeth, and ready for war. Why do we expect anything different here? The debris left over from the Cold War is like a uniform Islam is trying on in the Army surplus store; change the insignia and it fits.

How did it come to this? Have we uncovered a Weapon of Mass Destruction ? Has it been here all along in Radical Liberal dress?

CHAPTER ONE

The Inevitability of History

Hopes for the great communist society that Marx and Lenin had in mind could only arise from the destruction of all that now exists. The purpose of communism is to destroy. After nearly eighty years since the October Revolution they have introduced slavery and butchery on a scale unknown in mankind's history, and an economic order that can produce little more than a bare existence for generations ahead.

"For pure murderous evil there was never a force to compare with communism. The Nazis exterminated 11 million innocents... the Communist death toll surpasses 100 million," reported Jeff Jacoby in the Boston Globe. "Nazi power lasted from 1933 to 1945. The communist nightmare began in 1917 and continues to this day. Communism equals murder. Everywhere. Always."[1]

What is this philosophy that has produced so little, yet has snared more than a third of the world? Here is a brief outline of the complicated, so-called "scientific theory," that became the basis for the communist doctrine that for a time seemed destined to take over the world, and is still a threat.

Thesis, Anti-thesis, Synthesis — The Communist "Scientific" Theory

The German philosopher G. W.F. Hegel developed a special formula sometimes called the thesis-antithesis-synthesis dialectic to describe nature. This formula was noted by Karl Marx, who deducted that it also applied to man's struggles against political change.

Hegel had noted the dualism of the universe. There is man and woman, dark and light, up and down, to and fro, man and nature, etc., and these dialectics were constantly in a state of conflict.

28

Hegel deducted that God doesn't exist and the world is composed only of living matter. This idea is called materialism — hence the term "dialectical materialism." The main premise of materialism is atheism.

Karl Marx and his friend, Friedrich Engels, wrote that this dualism in the universe also applies to economics. The history of man was the result of "Economic Determinism" — man's effort to survive the basic creative force in human progress.

Some people have mistaken the mission of Karl Marx and his followers as economic in nature. Karl Marx is being presented in college classrooms as originator of an economic theory that is a viable alternative to capitalism. See any college curriculum.

However, like all materialists Marx's and Engels' mission was to gain power through ideological warfare. When Marx was asked what his object in life was, he replied, "To dethrone God and destroy capitalism!"[2] Marx and Hegel said that everything man does is merely the result of his desire to protect the mode of production he is currently using to secure the necessities of life. For example, when men decided that slavery was a good way to build buildings and produce crops, the dominant class instinctively moved to develop a society which protected the interest of slave owners. (thesis equals status quo).

The bourgeois or property class instinctively creates a society to protect their capitalistic interests (anti-thesis – enemy of the status quo). They believed that if some force comes along and changes the mode of production, say to machines, the dominant class will instinctively set about to create a different kind of society to protect the new economic order. Marx and Engels wrote that from the earliest times the mode of production and the mode of distribution have always produced two basic classes of people: those who owned the means of production (exploiters), and those who owned nothing and had to sell or trade their physical labor to survive (exploited).

This "to-and-fro" element of conflict between the thesis and the anti-thesis was identified by Marx and Engels as the basic force in history which prompts the evolution of society toward ever higher levels of achievement. Out of this conflict a new class (synthesis) emerges, which incorporates only the best of both classes. Man doesn't decide it. It just inevitably happens.

Outlaw Ownership of Private Property

They reasoned that this self-improving device of class struggles, (thesis, antithesis and synthesis) could be used in one final, terrible class struggle to permanently eliminate the thing that caused all the past conflicts in society — *private property.*[3]

If they could just use a final revolutionary class uprising to overthrow private property, class struggles would become unnecessary because there would be nothing to fight over, and *synthesis* with communism as the winner, would be complete.

They believed that family, marriage, the state and religion were all invented by the property class to protect their property. Religion was a man-made tool to teach the exploited class, humility, patience and long-suffering to endure the wrongs heaped upon him.

The fight against religion was to become one of the Party's most basic principles. Under communism, ethics and morality are based not upon religion but Party expediency. What the Party demands is moral and good. All else is immoral and bad. Religion is the opiate of the people, the destruction of which, is one of the most important tasks of the cultural revolution. They called prayer a social anesthetic for an intolerable environment

Class struggle, reasoned Marx, always produces a higher stage of civilization. He used an example — first came slavery, *(thesis),* then a class that wanted to abolish slavery (anti-thesis) a battle ensues and feudalism evolves *(synthesis)* which incorporates the best of both antagonists.

The struggle continued for thousands of years finally issuing forth a new *synthesis* called capitalism. Marx said that under the scientific law of revolution the capitalist class had already developed its own anti-thesis which he identified as the proletariat (the working class) which is striving to overthrow capitalism. Marx proclaimed that communism represented the new "synthesis" of the capitalist-proletariat struggle and the apex of all history.

The conflict would then cease and this new world would be the perfect and final society — stateless, classless, godless, where all property would be held in common and human activities would conform to the principle, "from each according to his abilities, to each according to his needs."

3. *There is no such thing as innate right or wrong.* To lie, is that wrong? Not for a good cause. Not if it serves my purpose. To kill, is that wrong? Not for a good cause. The end justifies the means. Ethics and morals are superficial and fraudulent.

4. *All religion must be overthrown because it inhibits the spirit of world revolution.* It is highly essential that all religion be methodically replaced with militant atheism. Religion keeps people from capturing the revolutionary spirit. It keeps people from lying and stealing and murder when the leaders demand it.

Scratch the Hide of Any Liberal

Do these concepts ring a bell? Scratch the hide of any Liberal. Their beliefs are the soul of dialectical materialism. They provide the reasoning for revolutionary violence, the reasoning to convert intellectuals to Liberalism, and make them, including those with great wealth, think that Liberalism is the great hope of the modem world.

Skousen notes that the most significant fallacy of the Communist philosophy is that problems can be solved by eliminating the institution from which the problems arise.

1. The problems of government – eliminate the government.
2. Moral problems – do away with morals.
3. Religious problems – do away with religion.
4. Marriage, home and family problems – do away with marriage, home, family.
5. Property rights – do away with property rights.
6. Equalizing wages – do away with wages.
7. Problems with money, markets and prices – do away with them.
8. Competition with production and distribution – prohibit competition.
9. The problems of modern society – destroy society.
10. Problems with free speech – eliminate free speech.

This is the philosophy that communism has sold to the world and that has such appeal to academia and which has been sold as a replacement for capitalism and free enterprise in the United States.

33

This Philosophy Is Not Dead — Not by a Long Shot

As early as February 3, 1996, the *Washington Post* reported that Russia's then president, Boris Yeltsin, had distanced himself from the reformist principles that his government had championed, purged the prominent reformers, and replaced them with hard-liners and warned of a United States military threat.

In typical communist fashion he balked at implementing any of the nuclear security and weapons inspection agreements announced by President Yeltsin and President Clinton at their summit meeting in May 1995.

Officials at the State Department, the White House and the Arms Control and Disarmament Agency said the mutual inspection and data exchanges on weapons and nuclear materials which the presidents said would happen — "are not about to happen."

So, what else is new? In all communist history they have entered into hundreds of agreements and signed treaties and have never honored a single one that didn't further their goal of world revolution. Never. Watch out NATO.

Yeltsin sent thousands of troops into Chechnya in December 1994, to crush a separatist movement. The Russian leadership was returning to the pattern of violence that has been its trademark from its very beginning. Russian forces have carried out dozens of attacks on towns and villages in Chechnya where civilians were the primary victims.

"Instead of seeing the strength of the state, we have just seen the cruelty of the state," wrote Otto Latsis, former advisor to Yeltsin. "The strength of the state shouldn't mean the ability to suppress and kill its own citizens. It should mean the ability to protect them." There is hope that the election of President Putin has issued-in a new level of relationship between the U.S. and Russia. We hopefully have lost an enemy and gained an ally. Don't hold your breath.

The Chinese Communists are Alive and Well

We have had more practical experience with the Chinese than we ever had with Russia. They are belligerent, warlike and "in your face" with what they plan to do. Even before they regained control of Hong Kong, talk was already turning to Taiwan. "Everyone knows Taiwan is a part of China," a spokesman for China's Ministry of Foreign Affairs told reporters. "There is no question."

The August 1997 *Reader's Digest*, a magazine that Tom Pauken said was about the only publication in America that did not actively support the Radical Left, said on page 54, "The collapse of the Soviet Union and its Eastern European clients shook China's leaders who noted the church's role in fostering the collapse. China's state-run press referring to Christianity, proclaimed, "If China does not want such a scene to be repeated in its land, it must strangle the baby while it is still in the manger."

The greatest champion of freedom around the world has been the church. When the church goes, so does freedom, and vice versa. The first thing China did in Hong Kong was move in troops. The world saw what they did to their own people in Tiananmen Square. Is there any sane person who does not believe they will do the same thing against the citizens of Hong Kong and the Taiwanese people if they get the chance? If they are communists, their own scientific theory says they must.

The Chinese president was reported in the press on July 2, 1997 as saying, "Without the leadership of the Communist Party of China *and the guidance of the scientific (Marxist-Leninist) theory*, it would be inconceivable for us to achieve national liberation, and build China into a strong and prosperous country." That was after he overlooked the theory and gave the Communist Party the credit for achieving the Hong Kong triumph.

We know they have a first class military, and are not afraid to use it against us as they did in Korea. They captured and kept in captivity over 7,000 American troops of which only 4,000 survived. The story of this period which gave us our first opportunity to see how Americans would respond to life in a communist society is presented in our chapter on Brainwashing attached as Appendix B.

The Chinese communists rattled their missiles in the direction of Taiwan just before the Taiwanese elections where they chose democracy and freedom. Our Seventh Fleet placed itself between China and Taiwan announcing once again, "You are not going to take another country!"

For those who have wondered about the difference between Russian communism and Chinese communism, they are the same philosophy. The difference has never been whether or not American capitalism must be buried. Their difference has been on our burial arrangements — how to go about doing us in.

Compared to China the Soviet Union was a Casper Milquetoast. The clever, intelligent, inscrutable Chinese were the ones who called us a "paper tiger," and sent a million troops into Korea against us. Read what they really think of Americans in Appendix B.

The 60s and 70s Radicals

Another problem —Tom Pauken in his book *The Thirty Years War* said that the 60s and 70s radicals are now in position to undermine the system they learned to hate long ago. President Clinton himself was a part of the radical left during his college days at Georgetown University and reportedly a colleague, or at least a supporter of, Tom Hayden head of Students for a Democratic Society called the most influential terrorist organization of the New Left in the 60s. Pauken, who knew him well, said Hayden saw himself as the Ho Chi Minh of America, was deadly serious about making a revolution in America, and had a strategic sense as to how to go about it.

We know President Clinton hated the Vietnam war. What else did he learn to hate? What is his vision for the future of America and the world?

The actions of President Clinton before he left office indicates he was turning his blindside to our history with China. He has given China most favored nation status, was investigated for soliciting money from them to insure his own election, and relaxed security in the White House to allow Chinese officials an open gangplank to enter as they chose. It is almost as though America was already theirs.

Many Americans are wondering what was going on there. Appointing communists to NATO, which required a unanimous vote to take any military action, played right into communist hands. It gave them a veto. Had we forgotten the United Nations so soon? What was President Clinton trying to do?

The communist timetable is behind schedule, but are we beginning to "fall into their hands"? How did it happen? You don't know? Most Americans don't have a clue. Krushchev said we wouldn't.

Weapon of Mass Destruction

The Radical Left communists, found they were not too popular in the United States, and in the 40s, looked for a place to hide in the Democratic Party. Some Democrats who didn't like what they were seeing began to abandon ship. Some went over to the Republicans, among them Ronald Reagan. Others went over to the Progressive Party following the, then, vice president Henry A. Wallace. The remaining are now found in the democrat stable as the Radical left, Liberals or Progressives, (a term generally associated with Communism) Call them what you will, they are brothers under the skin. They wave the flag and claim to be loyal patriotic Americans, but their actions show otherwise. It is no stretch to call Liberals the Weapon of Mass Destruction, which must be reined in if America is to survive.

One historian of the 60s and 70s, said intellectuals came down with the Liberal fever in college, which is now an epidemic, and from which they are not likely to ever recover. The Liberals are successors to the Progressives, Communists, Socialists and Radical Left of the 50s, 60s and 70s. Their theme song is, "our capitalist republic has to go." The Democrats of our fathers have been abandoned.

The results of a survey just released in the Fall of 2003 showed only about half of the Democrats could say they are proud of their country, i.e., patriotic, while 75 percent of Republicans said they were. The Liberals do not wish America well, and would trade our Capitalism for any other form of Socialist government.

The French, Germans and Arabs are alike in that they are all hard-nose Socialists and stick together. A Socialist is a communist who is not showing his gun. To understand them, think government control of everything, and hate capitalism, you will not be far wrong. Find Ann Coulter's books *Slander*, and *Treason*, and Mona Charen's *Useful Idiots*, and Laura Ingraham's *Shut Up and Sing*. They are all "right on" and each have the courage to speak up. The evidence is there.

Some historians drag the Clintons in. Before she met Bill, Hillary was a leader in the radical left in college, and was reportedly very close with the college communists. Bill debated and demonstrated for the Radical Left in college, and received an invitation to visit the Soviet Union, which he did…for a month…at a time when no American could get into Russia. You can see communist characteristics in each of them. The communist test of the truth is if it serves my self interest it is the truth. If it doesn't, it is a lie… "If it is not nailed down, it is mine… It takes a village to raise a child."

If it serves their best interest they can lie with a straight face and never give in. Bill didn't think it was wrong to lie to Hillary. She understands and forgives him. They both seem to be on a mission to remake America. Their indiscretions are just pot holes in the road.

CHAPTER TWO

Roots

The beginnings of communism can be traced directly to a landmark Sunday — January 22, 1905 — when the Tsar's Cossacks were set upon strikers in St. Petersburg, Russia, killing more than a thousand unarmed workers and wounding two thousand more.

A general strike spread to every major city in Russia, peasants revolted and before the year ended nearly three million persons had taken part in the rebellion. Mutiny even flared in the Navy.

The murdered strikers reportedly had not intended to revolt and launch any violence. Their petition was for a redress of grievances. Though they hated and feared the Cossacks and secret police they were loyal to the Tsar, whom they considered the father of the people. If they could only get past the armed guards which surrounded him and tell him the facts, they knew that justice would done. They didn't make it.

The Tsar tried to make concessions but it was too late. George Gapon, the Orthodox priest acting as their leader replied, "We no longer have a Tsar. A river of blood separates the Tsar from the nation. Long live the fight for freedom!"

The revolution of 1905 was suppressed but the seeds for the Bolshevik revolution were sown and on October 23, 1917, Russia was plunged into a civil war. The Tsar abdicated and a Provisional Government in Russia was established.

The Bolshevik leaders were nowhere in sight. Lenin was in exile in Switzerland, Trotsky was in exile in New York and Josef Stalin was in prison in Siberia. The Bolsheviks would never be able to take credit for the overthrow of the Tsar.

It was the generosity of the Provisional Government that allowed all political prisoners to be released from Siberia and political exiles allowed to come home.

When Lenin arrived in Petrograd he was welcomed by crowds of people. A military escort helped him to the roof of an armored car. Everyone was surprised when he denounced the Provisional Government and demanded a Communist Dictatorship of the Proletariat.

When Lenin struck out with his forces the Provisional Government suppressed the uprising and Lenin fled to Finland to save his life. When he felt it was safe to return, Lenin ordered Trotsky to have the Red Guard fire on the Winter Palace and seize the strongholds of the government. Under fierce attack the officials of the Provisional Government were captured.

The result was communist tyranny replaced the tyranny of the Tsar.[4] The masses of the people knew then that their dreams of a democracy were dead. The communists had overthrown the nearest thing to a democracy the Russians have ever known. Now the people would learn something about the Dictatorship of the Proletariat.[5]

Communism in America

The period from 1890 to 1910 saw the beginnings of a movement in America to make government the ally of the people against both big business and the hazards of accident and unemployment. Most of the ferment came from the "have-nots" making their political weight felt against the "haves" through labor agitation and unrest.

The language of the American protest was most often Marxist using tactics of mass pressure and goals ranging from reform to outright revolution. The extreme elements later were to form the Communist Party USA, on August 30, 1919.

Books and speeches of the period were filled with Karl Marx, William Morris and John Stuart Mill and audiences were ready to listen. Then in 1918 the United States became involved in WWI to "make the world safe for democracy," and America turned its attention to the war.

The Workers Party of America was formed in December,1921. The founding convention in New York City was organized and controlled by Communist Party leaders. The movement now had two sides to the communist coin — the underground communist

Party affiliated with the Third International in Moscow known as Number One and the Workers Party known as Number Two.

American communists of all varieties began to stream to Moscow, for meetings and to attend schools and as sight-seers. A delegation sailed in 1927 to celebrate the 10th anniversary of the Revolution. They returned to tell their comrades of this new land and made speeches all over the country: "Russia is the only real democracy on earth; working people are better off in Russia than in America."

Party leaders began to express themselves in more violent, revolutionary, bitter terms, shunning the cautious, evasive double talk of today's communists. They believed in violent revolution and said so. The Party was controlled as it is today by a very few, subject to the approval of the Kremlin, through the Comintern.

In 1929 Josef Stalin noted in a speech that the United States was heading toward a depression that would develop a revolutionary situation. *"It is essential that the American Communist Party be capable of meeting that historical moment and assuming the leadership of the impending class struggle in America. Every effort and every means must be employed in preparation for that, comrades. For that end we must work to liquidate factionalism and deviations in the Party. We must work for the re-establishment of unity in the Communist Party of America"* [6]

Americans had projected upon the events in Russia the feelings and attitudes formed by developments in this country. The idealism of the American communists drew its hope for human betterment from the institutions of American democracy. They didn't know what to make of the Russian communists and the Dictatorship of the Proletariat. The communism they envisioned bore slight resemblance to that which Lenin had established for the Union of Soviet Socialist Republics. Americans did not look upon themselves as serfs or slaves but as human beings with rights and, along with fellow workers, possessed of power.

Thus the American communist idealism, even though it chose the Soviet Union as its home land, was a product of the American tradition [7]

For the most part this dynamic American liberalism — more socialist than communist — stayed with change through democratic

41

means. It focused on the morally responsible individual who would not remain indifferent to exploitation and suffering and the needy individual whose powers and talents were being wasted and human rights ignored.

This continued to be the situation through the years of depression, war and Cold War and contributes to our misunderstanding of communism today. We look upon Russian actions and events in the Soviet Union through democratic eyes — as confusing as, understanding no Russian, talking to a Russian who understands no English.

Some anti-communists are persons attracted to communism as they believed it to be, who became disillusioned by its realities. Some understand communism on a name-calling kind of basis with many ignorances and fictions.

Then there are those, who through study and experience know exactly why communism was, and probably still is, a threat to human well-being.

A large bastion of people who still believe in the communist philosophy probably reside m the United States. Maybe they don't believe in communism, but they also don't believe in capitalism and freedom and remain a threat.

Even more dangerous are those who view communism as just another socialist political party, stick their heads in the sand and become vulnerable to the threat. That probably includes the majority ' of Americans.

CHAPTER THREE

The Cold War In Action
"Capitalism will die, sword in hand,
fighting in vain to beat back the oncoming
revolutionary proletariat."
— William Z Foster

The Cold War was not easy to understand. When WWII was over our ally in the Big War, the Soviet Union announced it was resuming its quest for world domination.

The Russians were big on Five Year Plans, and amazingly they told us about them. A 20-year plan in the 1940s, broken into five year segments, would be Europe, then Africa, then the masses of Asia, and then what figured to be about 1973, America would be ripe for the plucking and "world revolution will be an accomplished fact."

By the mid 1950s they had taken over from scratch and controlled over 900 million people — a third of the world. They had Europe, most of Africa and were working on the masses of Asia.

They had another 900 million people — another third of world — so confused they didn't know which side they were on. They did this with more success, less apparent trouble, than any government has ever controlled such large numbers of people.

In 1972, a year before we were to fall into their hands, a candidate for President of the United States would, astonishingly, join in demonstrations that a national enemy would defeat Americans in battle, and visit the capital and leader of that enemy nation, thus encouraging an enemy engaged in killing other Americans. (OK, I will save you some trouble looking it up; it was George McGovern.)

Americans need to consider why we were in Vietnam. We had to draw a line somewhere and say to the communist aggressors… "No more, you are not going to take another country."

Drawing the line in Vietnam may have been wrong — our secretary of defense at the time, Robert McNamara, now thinks so — but not fighting to win was certainly wrong.

Can you imagine a football team drawing a line across mid-field, and announcing to the opposition, "You play offense — we will play defense. We have no plans to score on you. We are only here to keep you from scoring."

You don't win football games that way and you certainly don't win wars that way. But that is what we did in Korea and Vietnam. It is what we did in the Cold War, in the Gulf War, and the war against Terrorism. and we are lucky to be here to tell about it. Sooner or later our luck is going to run out

These police actions were defensive in nature with no thought of offense. Ours was a containment policy. We were not there to take, any country or territory. We were there to keep them from taking it from others. Desert Storm was the same. When we had stopped Saddam Hussein and driven his troops back into Iraq, instead of going in and finishing him off, we stopped. History is beginning to prove we should have finished the job. One could make a case that we have lost all of our police actions. Our containment policies wind up containing us, and allowing our enemies to continue their aggressive ambitions.

Yes, the Cold War was a different kind of war. Russia did not line up its great army, navy and air force and attack anybody, except their own people. or later in Afghanistan. The strategy always was to soften up the target, divide and conquer.

The moles and agents spoke the local language fluently and became part of the community. Their mission was to discredit, drive a wedge between the people and any feeling of loyalty they might feel toward their country or any institution.

The moles would be underground, and their status not known to anybody even their families. Our intelligence sources tell us the moles were instructed to infiltrate the government at all levels, the schools, communications apparatus such as print, radio, television and movies, churches, big business and even the military, keep a low profile, and move into responsible positions.

The agitators would be assigned to latch onto a cause that could be used to arouse the people, and with other agitators, infiltrate both sides of the argument. The cause would not be important, the argument was the objective. It could be anything. Just keep the conflict going.

Any government official can tell you how two or three determined individuals can build a mountain out of a molehill, can cause people to do things as drastic as burning and looting their own city.

It doesn't take many. You could fit the Communists who took over Russia in 1917 into the average college football stadium — less than 25,000 people. Small countries reportedly have been taken over by as few as 250 people.

When the conflict got so big it threatened to topple the government they would propose a truce, set down at the bargaining table and propose a coalition government.

In 18-months or less the Russian, or preferably a satellite country's troops, would be invited in to take over without firing a shot. The country and its infrastructure were still intact, not all torn up by war. The troops lined up all the opposition leaders of the country, and had themselves a little liquidation party. Most often the victims just disappeared never to be heard from again. The communists have murdered over 100 million people — not in battle but in their definition of peace.

This is not contrived. If we protested they would say it was an internal affair. After all Russia didn't have any troops in there until they were invited. It was a civil matter, and if it did turn into a fight it was a civil war.

The Vietnam War Gave Communism a Great Cause

They had the same plan for us here in America. We gave them great causes to exploit in Korea and Vietnam. Choosing places like Korea and Vietnam to draw the line in retrospect was unfortunate. You don't draw the line where you can't win. You don't tie your own troops' hands behind their backs and expect to win.

Americans finally caught on to what our diplomats in the State Department were doing, and saw Vietnam for what the communists considered it — another country in their plan for world domination.

45

To the people in Vietnam and to the world that received only propaganda, and not the big view, it was just a civil war, that the U.S. butted into as an aggressor.

The U.S. soldier in Vietnam was at a serious disadvantage. The VietCong army was scattered throughout the countryside living in the villages often right under American noses. Oftentimes they were women and children. It was not uncommon after a firefight where Viet Cong were killed, to find people among the dead, like the woman who did the laundry on the base, who the Americans knew very well.

A marine major friend of mine said that the young marine or soldier would get off the plane and ask, "Where is the enemy?" He would be told, "Don't worry; you will know soon enough." The enemy soldiers would be mixed right in with the citizenry, in civilian clothes, using the women and children as his cover.

A machine gun burst would take out a few Americans, and the enemy fire identified as coming from a certain building. Mortar fire was directed at the building. Sometimes they had to blow up a couple of buildings to get the right one.

My nephew, Paul Gregory, said after his tour in Vietnam, it was not uncommon for the VietCong to place a booby trap in a baby's diaper, and send him out to get candy from a group of American soldiers, blowing up their own baby in order to kill three or four Americans. Their baby was just a fragment of humanity; if this one is killed we can get another.

The TV next evening in America would show the women and children "killed by American fire." Our media did not have access to the communist side but they had access to ours, and they took advantage of it — no matter what damage it was doing to our men's morale, and to our side. They didn't seem to know, or care.

All in the name of America's right to know. If you didn't know what the war was about it could be very discouraging. Is it any wonder that the man on the street was confused — that the idealistic students who had only the communist line about what we were doing over there, were confused?

If there is any doubt who orchestrated, and controlled those demonstrations get some old videos and hear the chants, "Go, go, Ho Chi Minh" and hear Americans actually cheering for an enemy that was engaged in killing other Americans and waving VietCong flags. Is it any wonder that the young soldiers, sailors and airmen we sent over there — with no clear idea of why they were there — were confused and hurt?

I agree with the Radical Left — the Vietnam War was one of the darkest times in American history — but for an entirely different reason. It was a time when Americans were duped into becoming a part of an enemy's war against America.

How Demonstrators Are Recruited

Have you ever wondered how the murderous communists could recruit American students in such large numbers to come out to their meetings and throw rocks at the police? J. Edgar Hoover, founder and long-time leader of the Federal Bureau of Investigation, who collaborated with his agents to write a book, *Masters of Deceit*, gave us some insight as to how it was done.

A young woman stands on the sidewalk. A student carrying books comes out of the classroom. "Pardon me," the young woman says. "Would you like the war to end?" The appeal is attractive. The young woman continues. "We have a petition to the President asking for the war to be stopped to save thousands of American lives." The student looks at the petition. It contains nothing communist. No hammer or sickle or mention of Russia. It is just a statement that "We the undersigned believe that the war should be ended. You can help a lot by signing."

The student signs, and so do thousands of others. Party members are on a hundred college campuses, on street corners, at the bus stops. Sign here please. Won't you send a telegram or write a letter? Here is a sample all fixed up. Would you like a leaflet? Won't you call your congressman or senator or the President's office? Come to our rally tonight? Write a letter to the newspaper? Is your club meeting soon? Have it pass a resolution. Your pastor can help. Have him call a protest meeting.

The pressure is tabulated in thousands of letters, resolutions, and telegrams, a hundred times the total number of all the Communist Party members in the United States. The pressure grows. Thousands show up at mass meetings, rallies, demonstrations and other exploitation staging points. "American's young men are being killed." "Our bombs are killing women and babies." "Wire the President. Stop the war." "Where is America's conscience?"

Sojourns, treks, pilgrimages, motorcades, encampments, converge on a selected spot, like Washington, D.C. — they arrive by carpool, trains, rented buses, battered old trucks, hitchhiking. An operational headquarters is set up with a freedom sounding name like "Liberty House" or "Inspiration Center." Prayers are said by communists who do not believe in prayer.

The media steps in. "Washington was stirred today by thousands of students demanding an end to the Vietnam War." The television news donates a few sound bites, and pictures of dead babies killed by Americans.

Did those demonstrators love their country? Maybe they did, but not enough to resist the propaganda at least in the beginning. I believe they should have seen enough in the intervening years to love it more now, but history is showing us they haven't changed, and are not behaving differently. But if some of the blood of the 58,000 Americans who were lost in Vietnam is not on their hands, at least they helped to make our servicemen's sacrifice in vain. The communists had their war in Vietnam and they won it — in the streets of America — with American fighters and American free speech and assembly, aided and abetted by a willing press. We fought for a tie — a containment of the communists — and wound up with a defeat.

The duped and presumably innocent demonstrators recruited to communist causes were as lost to America, to Freedoms' cause, as if they had been captured or wounded or killed.

Communist Talking Points and Come Along Points

A discussion with a communist always begins with legitimate American interests, such as peace, lower taxes, higher wages, better housing, social security for seniors, higher farm income, a balanced budget - items desired by most of the people. To support these aims is not to be a communist. They are party "talking points." The "come along" points are the objective.

A discussion may start about the high price of gasoline, better working conditions on the second shift, equal pay for women, save the whales, or the grasshoppers, or the death rate among Eskimos, but will end with an endorsement of peace, amnesty for a convicted communist criminal, or the end of the war in Vietnam.

Hoover reports some "come along" points that were actually attained. Look closely at how the adoption of these demands as conceived by the Party distort their true meanings, and aid the communist cause.[8] At the time he wrote his book, in 1958 here were some communist objectives:

"Restore the Bill of Rights" which means in communist language elimination of legal opposition to communism, stopping all prosecution of communists and granting amnesty to those behind bars.

"Repeal the Draft Law" means curtailing our defense effort and allowing them to become stronger.

"Increase trade with the Soviet Bloc" means selling materials that could be used by the communist nations for armaments.

"Restore academic freedom" means we should permit the official teaching of communist doctrine in all schools and allow communists to infiltrate teaching staffs.

Note the word "restore" which means freedom is already gone and the party stands for its return. The "come along" points just mentioned have all become the law of the land. The communist objective is that America be rendered helpless to protect herself. The Party searches American life for agitation points, the arrest of an African-American, the eviction of a family, a miscarriage of justice, corporate downsizing, dismissal of a teacher, a shooting or beating by a police officer.

Some unfortunately do reflect mistakes or blemishes in American society. Lenin teaches — all are to be twisted by the party into agitational items. "Today *he* is being persecuted. Tomorrow will be your turn. Join us and we will fight together."

The deception is, that the communists hold themselves out as fighting with us for a common democratic heritage. The truth is, they are fighting to gain the support of non- communist groups to further socialism. As Lenin instructed, "Seize allies everywhere."

Watching all this, I must confess to coming to believe Khrushchev who proclaimed on U.S. television that our grandchildren would live under Socialism.

I was wrong. American democracy is not dead yet. The Cold War ostensibly is over or at least we hope it is. Recent elections in Russia have shown that Russian communism may not be dead, but our officials and press are showing an alarming complacency.

Communism is not dead. The bear is in hibernation. There are plenty of people here in the U.S. who still believe that capitalism has to go. Probably the only place in the world where you can still learn that communism or Marxism is a viable economic alternative to capitalism is in American college classrooms. I have been there and listened to that tripe. I heard an economics professor say, "If you took capitalism to its ultimate conclusion it would always wind up in a depression or in war." That came straight from the communist handbook.

Cold War End a Communist Strategic Retreat ?

Is it possible that the end of the so-called Cold War is nothing but a communist strategic retreat? Lenin taught the approach to psychological warfare must be varied, flexible and constantly subject to change. He said it is like climbing an unexplored mountain. "We cannot renounce beforehand the idea that at times we might have to go in zigzags, sometimes retracing our steps, sometimes abandoning the course once selected and trying various others…two steps forward…one step back. Those who do not understand this fail to understand Marxism."

Lenin might say if he were here, "Those who believe the Cold War is over fail to understand Marxism." One of the top candidates for president in Russia in 1996, Gennady Zyuganov, vows a return to communism, and the return of the old Soviet Union. Further he states that Russia will resume its policy of "collecting nations." Meaning, of course, a return to its quest for world domination in their constitution. They say Communism will not work unless all of us are doing it. Or that Communism is a victim of bad leadership, and deserves another chance. I say to the communist, "Try Freedom. You may like it."

As the Cold War was winding down, Russia began to allow their sailors to come to American for world regattas without their interpreter. One of the first Russian teams to come to the Dallas area for the Soling World Championships direct from Kiev, was impressed with a Texas bumper sticker, and tee shirts designed to keep down litter in the streets which reads, "Don't Mess With Texas." A female scorekeeper had a time translating that into Russian.

CHAPTER FOUR

We Have Seen the Enemy and He Is Us

Communism — a riddle wrapped in a puzzle,
wrapped in an enigma
— Winston Churchill

Looking back my first realization that something was amiss in America came in the late 1940s after the end of WWII, when as a young Navy careerman, I noticed something strange happened. All "Know Your Enemy" training sessions were abruptly halted, never to be resumed.

The major mission of the United States military is training. When we are not fighting we are training to fight. An important part of that training is knowing who and why we are fighting.

When our enemy was Germany and Japan, "Know Your Enemy" training sessions were held every week on a regularly scheduled basis. Every man in service during those times knew the name of every top German and Japanese leader, their backgrounds and as much as we could, how they would fight.

We knew about the Japanese Emperor and how the Japanese soldier, sailor and airman would gladly lay down their lives for him as a religious duty. We knew why we must keep the Emperor in place or no lasting peace after the war could be assured. We knew the German soldier and the Japanese soldier, and what we could expect in combat.

When the big war was over, it soon became clear that our old enemy, the Soviet Union, was back on the horizon with the revived mission of burying capitalism and conquering the world.

The military started to teach its people about the Soviet Union, their strategy and tactics and how they would fight. We were told about world communism — how it started, its objectives and leaders and tried to make some sense of their position which vacillated all over the place. Ask a question and get back a riddle.

We learned about communism in the United States, about their plan for world conquest and how we fit into the scheme. We learned about their five-year plans and how the long range plan introduced in the late 1940s, would start with Europe, then Africa, then Asia and how we were to fall into their hands like a ripe plum. It figured to be about 1973.[9] You do remember what came to pass in 1973? Don't lose that thought.

Communist Briefings Halted

Our briefings were abruptly halted and to my knowledge were never resumed. No more briefings on communism — at least to all the troops. We wondered what was up but never found out. Major General Edwin Walker was drummed out of the Army for continuing his educational programs.

As a result our troops would often be sent into Korea and Vietnam with no clear idea of why they were there — except for the broad objective of "fighting Communism" or "we were invited in." Vietnam veteran and intelligence officer Thomas W. Pauken would write after the Vietnam War, "It seemed to me America hadn't paid enough attention to the objectives of our enemy and how they planned to achieve them."[10]

Legislation From the Bench

FBI Director J. Edgar Hoover, was a man with a mission, the protecting of the country from communists. He had a mountain of information on file with what became known as the "Political Activities of American Citizens Helping Communists." Liberals called it Hoover's "gross excesses." He was tough, but effective.

The liberal revolutionists hated him. After Hoover died, new regulations were written which barred law enforcement surveillance and infiltration unless there was a "reasonable indication," the communists were ready to resort to violence, (interpreted to mean were carrying guns). A major source of intelligence was dried up.

Freedom of speech, and freedom of assembly were in case after case made available to the communists by Supreme Court edict. We would place our freedoms and way of life in great jeopardy in the name of the radical left's right to foment revolution in the United States, and the Supreme Court's propensity to assist them.

A Supreme Court decision would change the legal definition of treason, and allow a movie star, Jane Fonda, and a presidential candidate, George McGovern, to visit, and thus offer encouragement to the enemy leaders in Vietnam engaged in killing American soldiers. It freed the communists to lead American students in demonstrations against the Vietnam War. In previous wars such actions were treason and punishable by death. Security and loyalty were not primary legal considerations in the Cold War period.

The Supreme Court under Earl Warren, swayed by liberal claims of witch hunts and communists under every bed, and claims that innocent Americans were having their reputations and careers ruined, would remove judicial restraints, and either dis-allow a large proportion of anti-Communist legislation, or neutralize its effectiveness.

Indoctrinated lawyers, along with the ACLU always eager to file a case that upset the status quo, filed lawsuits on behalf of the communists. They have now succeeded in removing virtually every law that we had to combat the menace. Our law enforcement, CIA and FBI are virtually neutralized, and out of business insofar as the revolution is concerned. Some analysts say the Constitution as presently interpreted by the judiciary is no longer able to provide for the common defense against adversaries from within like communists or Terrorists.

The 9/11 Commission of 2004, formed to learn where we went wrong at the twin-towers, seemed shocked that the FBI and CIA weren't talking to each other, when in reality it was against the law, as interpreted by the Supreme Court. Present laws originally passed or changed in the 60s and 70s, are skewed to the benefit of the guilty, and virtually useless where national defense is an issue. It is within the power of the Congress to clean them up, but no legislators have the courage to take on the liberal courts. The 9/11 Commission would be well advised to look into Supreme Court files of the 50s. They might be surprised at what they would find.

Earl Warren Releases Professors Teaching Violent Overthrow of U.S.

The Supreme Court under Earl Warren released and had returned to their classrooms at Harvard University a dozen or so professors who had been turned in by members of the Communist Party and students for teaching and advocating the overthrow of the United States by force and violence. The grounds — that they had not actually used guns.

Words Are As Dangerous As Cannon Balls

Words were indeed a weapon of the communists and were harmful. Language was the weapon used to drive wedges, agitate, gain control, and keep order over the 900 million people that would come under their iron fist, and create confusion with another 900 million people who had not decided which side they were on.

Words ultimately would involve our troops in Korea and Vietnam and be the basis of the brainwashing of our prisoners of war in Korea, which we will describe.[11]

William Bennett said, the media urges "individuals to be precisely the kind of people whom nobody would want as an employee, boss, colleague, friend, brother or spouse." The media pushes the corruption of our society because there is money to be made from it

A Supreme Court decision would change the legal definition of treason which allowed a movie star and a presidential candidate in 1972 to visit, and thus offer encouragement to the enemy leaders in Vietnam, engaged in killing American soldiers. It would free the communists to lead American students and intelligentia in demonstrations against the Vietnam War. In previous wars such actions were treason and punishable by death.

Our freedom of speech and freedom of assembly, were in case after case, made available to the communists by our court system to be used against us. We would place our freedoms and way of life in great jeopardy in the name of the "Radical Left's" rights to agitate and foment revolution in the United States.

"Ronald Reagan was right when he attacked our no-win strategy. We fought for a tie and ended up with a defeat," wrote Pauken.[12]

Communism Up Front With Their Plans

Fortunately this enemy told us what they were going to do, chapter and verse. Sometimes temporary strategy hid their ultimate intentions but during the past 80 years they have never veered one iota from their long-range objectives. The problem has been our own refusal to believe them. We don't believe they mean what they say and therefore their threats are ignored.[13]

The material was so wide-spread it was non-classified intelligence. Admittedly over-simplified, they would target a country, go in with a few agitators and attempt to drive a wedge between the people and the government. If they could get the people demonstrating in the streets and the police could be brought in — great! If they could arrange counter-demonstrations — much greater. If they could get the media to report on it — greater still! Especially if the story was sympathetic to the demonstrators and unsympathetic to the government

The objective was to get the populace aroused. After a few brushes with the police or troops, the demonstrators would be so angry toward their government they would almost be ready to take up arms against it. (We could see this in action when American college students rioted against the Vietnam War, shouting "Ho, Ho, Ho Chi Minh" while waving Viet Cong flags.) As the people got more angry the demonstrations grew bigger.

Since the communists were on both sides of the argument they could propose a truce, and if the disagreement was big enough, a coalition government. Since they were on both sides of the argument, after a few months it would be easy to ask for aid from the Soviet Union and the troops could come in and take over the country without a shot. This wasn't an invasion — they were invited. The country's infrastructure of buildings, roads, railroads and airports were not all tom up but remained intact. A great way to run a war, you will have to admit.

This is the plan they had for us. They may yet achieve it. The Cold War may be over, but the bear is not dead. He is merely in hibernation.

Do Their Plans Work?

One by one they picked off countries and continents until in the 1950's they controlled over a third of the world, over 900 million people, and had another third so confused they didn't know which side they were on. They did this over and over again.

The United States was the bastion of capitalism and communism, by its very definition, was vowed to destroy us. We were a target and a center for their agitation and propaganda from about 1917. The only reason America did not become the center of communism in the world, instead of Russia, was that the convenient Russian Revolution in 1917 gave them control of Russia first and they set up shop there.

There was no doubt that the United States was their major target, the destruction of which was their reason for being.

U. S. a Major Target for Propaganda

They circulated their instructions openly in the U.S. to their underground moles, sympathizers and fellow-travelers through communist publications which could be bought on the news stands in America. It was not against the law to spread their poison, so they were very open about it.

They used what Hoover called Aesopian language in which the point is not directly stated but must be inferred by the reader. Such expressions as democracy, equality, freedom, and justice are Aesopian devices to impress non-communists. They clothe themselves with everything noble, good and inspiring to exploit these ideals to their own advantage. J. Edgar Hoover wrote, "The communist is not an angel of mercy, ministering to the weak, oppressed and wounded but a menacing demon spattered with blood wielding a hammer and sickle of iron."[14]

Our media, in an attempt to be fair and objective would pick up their propaganda and spread it through our press and electronic media, with hardly a hint as to where it came from or that it might be harmful to America. The writers and editors either didn't know what might be harmful or they didn't care.

Counterspy Herb Philbrick, for a time the head of Agitation/Propaganda for the Communist Party USA said he didn't need 25,000 people in his pocket to get his stuff into the newspaper. "All I needed was two, the night editors of AP and UP." Not to say they were communists or even a security risk. To give them the benefit of the doubt, they were busy people who may have been suspicious and wondered about the crazy communists, but didn't see the harm in it.

Communist party members remained mostly underground, doing their dirt through front organizations with patriotic sounding names. They recruited moles sympathetic to their causes. and made maximum use of phrases such as, "I don't believe in what you say, but will fight to the death for your right to say it." This phrase, reportedly first seen in the communist press, became the hallmark of our freedom of speech, and a spear point for communist propaganda.

The moles worked underground to get into positions of power so they would be ready to take over when the time came. With Aesopian language that always talked about freedom and democracy and solving the problems that plagued our system of government, (which they carefully pointed out, in case you missed them), the communists capitalized on the "idealism of youth," and the "intelligentsia" (their phrases), loosely interpreted as those educated or indoctrinated beyond their intellect who could be sold on anything critical of the establishment

The communists openly instructed party members, fellow travelers and dupes to use the avenues of communication to soften up and corrupt youthful attitudes about patriotism, religion, their parents, police, military, politicians or any form of constituted authority.

Their efforts were so successful that it is hard to believe that we live in the same America that existed in the 1940s.

The Results Are In

The prevailing attitudes in America in 2004 among too many people are that patriotism is for nerds. Religion is widely disrespected and disparaged, especially by the media which reports with disgust about the "religious right," and pro-lifers are looked upon with scorn. Couples living together without benefit of clergy is an accepted lifestyle with the same benefits as married couples. Drug use is commonplace even in grade school. Same-sex marriages are becoming acceptable and in some states legal. As fashions change, "we abhor, then we accept, then we embrace." We are embracing any and everything.

Too many children have no respect at all for their parents, and have come to believe that the police take bribes and plant evidence to trap innocent Americans, and politicians are all crooks that can be bought. They believe that if you have enough money you can get away with the most heinous of crimes, that the military is run by idiots and fools, and a military career is unthinkable. Nothing, not even freedom, is worth dying for. We seem to have lost all perception of right and wrong or of what might be harmful to other Americans.

These Attitudes Promulgated By the Media

Where did we get those attitudes? From what we see and hear. Compare the old movies and sitcoms on television such as *I Love Lucy, Leave it to Beaver, Ozzie and Harriet,* the old westerns, musicals such as *Singing in the Rain,* and hundreds of others which had no profanity or sexual innuendoes, and were, and are, great character builders and still great movies today. They aren't making them anymore. Hollywood once made movies that respected these values.

The industry for more than forty years followed an explicit standard when it came to portrayals of organized religion and the clergy. The official standard stated: "No film or episode may throw ridicule on any religious faith; ministers of religion shall not be portrayed as comic characters or villains; ceremonies of any definite religion should be carefully and respectfully handled."[15]

Now you would be hard-pressed to find one character-building movie on the screen or on television. There are no movies that do not show ministers as comic or criminal characters. All sitcoms are filled with profanity, sex, violence and a condescending attitude toward the ignorant public, who can be given anything because the public is too dumb, and too weak to demand something decent. All in the name of freedom of speech. I still see the talking head on television shouting, "Don't you get it? We don't care!"

There are no gatekeepers at the zoo. Bob Garfield a columnist at *Advertising Age* said, "Aside from saying that Advil is better than aspirin, you can get away with anything now."

What would happen if the adversary culture the communists and radical left support actually pervaded our whole society? "It would look pretty much like what we have now — a culture that celebrates impulse over restraint, notoriety over achievement, rule breaking over rule keeping and any kind of incendiary expression over minimal civility."[16]

Our laws protect us from garbage in the streets, but garbage in the minds of our young people is gloriously OK. We have maximum freedom of speech and assembly but virtually no national character.

Remember that communists had clear objectives to soften up the people and the results show that they did. When America called upon its young adults to take up arms to stop communism, many skipped off to Canada, burned their draft cards, or went into the streets to cheer that the communists would prevail over American soldiers. Young women burned their bras and engaged in "free sex" in public, rock music laced with lyrics against the war sang the praises of drug use, free love and rebellion against any constituted authority. College professors joined students in their protests and vowed to close down a university and call a national strike unless we stopped the war or withdrew from Indochina.[17]

Slogans like "Nothing is worth dying for," "Better Red than dead," "I don't believe in what you say, but I will fight to the death for your right to say it" played right into the hands of those who wanted to make this country a Russian satellite.

"A society that badly needs a serious discussion about civility seems determined not to have it." said John Leo. "...all attempts at reform must come to terms with the 1960s generation and its belief that (changing) social forms and norms are hypocritical masks for (keeping) the status quo."[18]

What we need but what we are not likely to get is zero tolerance for messages and tactics aimed at degrading our society and supporting the aims and objectives of an enemy vowed to destroy us.

CHAPTER FIVE

Movie Industry Blacklist and the Hollywood Ten

When the HUAC (House Un-American Activities Committee) turned its hearings from government employees to Hollywood it hit pay dirt. As a result of the hearings approximately 250 stars and writers were fired and blacklisted by the industry. Ten writers were jailed for a year and became known as the Hollywood Ten.

The American Movie Classics (AMC) cable channel presented a 90-minute program on the Hollywood Blacklist on February 27, 1996. While sympathetic to the stars and writers, the program nevertheless gave a graphic picture of what the stars were doing through interviews and their appearance before the House Un-American Activities committee. The charges against them were disloyalty (susceptibility to the philosophical or moral enticements of an enemy state or a competing ideology) and of aiding or participating in communist causes and/or of actually being members of the Communist Party themselves.

The February 27 program listed many of the movies (not all) written by, directed by and/or acted in by the blacklisted people. I will not use any of their names, though a movie goer will know them all. You would be shocked at who they were. It is a matter of public record.

At the beginning of the program one of the Hollywood Ten freely admitted they all wrote social, political and opinion-altering issues into every one of their films. He lamented that they could not come right out with the communist agenda but had to hide their message, in such things as dialogues about racism, anti-Semitism, and against the establishment.

The writers' communist leanings were clear in the program. They admitted them. Some of the writers were even asked in interviews and conversations which they would support in the event of a war between the United States and the Soviet Union. Many chose the Soviets.

However when asked by the congressional committee if they "were, or had ever been, a member of the communist party," everyone of the Ten evaded the question. It was clear they had read and understood the communist pamphlet on how to defend yourself when arrested and questioned described in Chapter 7 of this book. They attacked the committee and questioned their right to hold the hearings, said the committee was using Gestapo tactics and had no Constitutional right to ask that question. When the moderator demanded they answer the question they continued to disrupt the proceedings until the moderator had them removed.

It was interesting to see the stars and writers engage in the communist practices of *Informing* and *Self-criticism* during the hearings. After the hearings they withdrew from one another much as described in Appendix B on Brainwashing.

Examples of the Communist "Line"

A television series during that period, *I Led Three Lives*, was based on the life of Herb Philbrick, counterspy for the FBI and the head of Agitation-Propaganda for the Communist Party USA. I was privileged to meet him and hear him speak. His stories would curl your hair. (It made mine come out.)

He said, "You want to be brainwashed? You don't have to go to Russia. Just go to your nearest movie theater or watch television for thirty minutes any night."

Philbrick said to look for material that degraded fathers, the police, religious leaders, government leaders, military leaders and applauded or glorified anti-establishment behavior — anything that drove a wedge between you and American values.

He described a movie written by, directed by and acted in by blacklisted people. It was a Navy picture during the Korean War where the captain was complaining all film-long about being called to active duty.

In one particularly bloody scene a young sailor had his arm blown off at the armpit. The captain visited the sailor in the sick bay, and said, "Maybe you are the lucky one. You will get to go home."

Philbrick stationed himself in the lobby and asked people what they thought of the fllm. All said, "It was great!" Then he asked,

"Would you want your son (or would you want to) join the Navy?" He got all negative responses, which in his job as head of propaganda for the communist party, were exactly the answers he wanted.

The News Media Seems to Believe Its Reason for Being Is to Attack America and Its Institutions

A recent example of how you can influence the public's attitude toward the presidency was aired on the CBS television news-magazine *48 Hours*, Thursday evening March 7, 1996. The thrust of the entire hour-long program was the problems a Presidential candidate endures during his campaign.

Media consultants showed how they dug up dirt on candidates and sold it to competing candidates. Dan Rather and his panel of "experts" were decrying the fact that we don't get statesman like Washington, Lincoln and Roosevelt the way we used to "before 1948."

The panel recognized that the attitude the newsmen take toward their profession now, as opposed to the days when they simply reported the news, and stayed out of the dirty tricks and analysis business, contributed to the problem. However, they seemed to have no idea how it got that way. As Krushchev said, "You won't know how it happened."

Over and over industry leaders who would make excellent statesmen stated on the program they did not "need the aggravation" of running for the office of president.

Toward the end of the program Rather asked some kids in the audience if they had ever wanted to be president. All said no, except one young lad who said, "I used to want to be President, but not anymore."

The U2 Spy Plane Incident

I am not picking on Rather, but I recall vividly when the Soviet Union shot down one of our U2 spy planes and captured its pilot, Francis Powers. The young newsman was incensed to learn that America had spy planes and particularly berated President Eisenhower for not immediately leaving the golf course to answer to hostile newsmen.

I remember as a young chief petty officer screaming at my TV screen, "Shut your mouth, you idiot! Don't you know you are on national TV and the Russians are listening. That is our President you are publicly insulting!" He didn't seem to understand that in a war with a closed country like Russia, with complete freedom of access to our society, we have to do what we can to learn about what they are doing, any way we can. He was defending and taking the side of our enemy.

The reporters seemed to have no understanding then, and I don't believe it crosses their minds now, what may be harmful to their country. Rather was probably among those Vice President Spiro Agnew had in mind when he asked. "Who are these people on television every night who are telling you what to think? What do you know about them? Who elected them?"

It is not just Rather. There are hundreds, or more likely thousands, just like him. I want to make it perfectly clear that I am not accusing the press or anybody else of being communists or even communist sympathizers. I just wish they would use their powers of persuasion in more positive ways. If you can't help us, don't help that "bear."

What Happened to the Blacklisted Actors and Hollywood Ten

If you have seen any movies, you have seen one or more movies written by all of the Hollywood Ten since they served their sentences. All have controversial political themes, which are almost never favorable to America, capitalism and freedom. Dalton Trumbo won two Oscars writing such themes under an alias, before he came out of the closet.

One of the musicians blacklisted in the 1960s, Pete Seeger, was presented with a Kennedy Center Honors medal in 1994. One of his books, a commentary on the blacklists, was made into a movie and shown to the kids on *Sesame Street*.

After the media had sufficiently altered public opinion, by explaining it to us dummies that the HUAC hearings and industry blacklisting was "a black day in American history," the writers and actors came out of the closet, one by one, and their movies are on television every night. They explain to us that the Ten who went to jail, were heroes who lived in the darkest days in American history, when freedom of speech was almost lost.

However the attitudes the communists helped to develop which are threatening to destroy America are alive and well and picking up steam. The Academy Awards celebration has always been a platform for "piling on" right wing and conservative candidates and the 1996 program of March 25, 1996, was no exception. If the assault laws included verbal abuse a number of movie stars and television commentators would be serving time.

Steven Spielberg in his introduction of Kirk Douglas who would receive an honorary Oscar, said Douglas had tramped all over the "Blacklist" during his career and showed many clips of his social issues and ideological themes.

Have you ever seen a movie or television show that mentions the Blacklist that does not make the blacklisted people out to be heroes? The same can be said of Vietnam demonstrators. It is a sad day when our dupes, traitors and turncoats are heroes, and our patriots who stood tall and true are spat upon.

The crusade against communists which would last nearly a decade effectively drove the American Communist Party underground and demoralized most of its fronts. In the last years college students would make a game of it and reply "Yeah, man!" to the cheers of his friendly audience when asked, "Are you a communist?"[19] The McCarthy era, the only time when communism in America has been seriously challenged, died not by political opposition, but by ridicule.

The Chet Huntley Caper

In the late 1950s, as a member of the Commanding Officers' Dallas Naval Air Station speaking team, I was assigned to make a speech to the Longview Texas Rotary Club. Longview is in the center of the East Texas oil fields. The team, by invitation, carried the Navy message to the public. A reserve pilot on two-weeks active duty, was to fly me over to Longview, about 125 miles. As luck would have it, the plane was down for a maintenance problem, and it was 9:30 AM before I learned no other plane was available.

Did you know that a VW beetle can fly? Traveling east in a 20mph crosswind, I don't think all four wheels hit the ground until I pulled into the hotel parking lot in Longview. I scurried into the hotel ballroom, as the meeting was being called to order, and was seated next to the podium. The chairman struck his big bell as hard as he could, just as my bottom was finding the seat.

The ballroom was jammed; the chairman said, 250 people. My nerves were tight as guitar strings, but the bell loosened me up. The group was complimented on its positive attitude, because they thanked God for the meal before they tasted it, and blessed their speaker before they heard him. I was hot. I laid my notes aside and made the best speech I have ever made, before or since. In the middle of the speech, an old gentleman in the back of the room had a fainting spell.

We had three pre-approved speeches as I recall, International Communism, Communism in the USA, and Americanism. I was to talk on Number two. I talked on a little bit of all three, and opened the floor to Q&A.

The first question set the tone. "If a chief in the Navy knows all this stuff, how come our government doesn't know it?" I assured them our government did know, but we didn't want to start a shooting war.

The next question was about the movie Industry Black List and Hollywood Ten. This subject was hush-hush, and had not been released. The questioners wanted to know if there was such a blacklist, and who was on it. The liberal Peter Jennings of the day was Chet Huntley on TV News every night, sponsored by Texaco. The questions quickly got to the point. "Is Chet Huntley on that list?" I paused, reflecting on whether I should answer, and then I nodded affirmatively. My instructions were not to bring up the subject, but if it came up, to answer it. I learned later that someone in the audience had wired Texaco, and told them to get that SOB off the air, or "we won't sell you another drop of oil."

The next day my CO called me to his office and showed me what looked like a seven-page Western Union Telegram from Chet Huntley, protesting his innocence. The CO, a Navy four-striper captain, wired back, asking "If you are so innocent, why don't you sue?" Huntley's reply, "They don't have any money." Meaning, he would lose the lawsuit.

Bottom line — after a few weeks the oil guys settled down, Chet Huntley, hopefully a little bit chastened, kept his job, and Texaco kept selling gas. The guy who fainted recovered. My CO said I did just right.

The Hollywood Ten

The Hollywood Ten were accused of having ties with the Communist Party, by the House Un-American Activities Committee, or for refusal to testify, or for challenging the committee's right to interrogate them about their political beliefs.

They were sentenced for up to a year in prison for contempt of Congress and Blacklisted by the HUAC and the movie industry. Some went underground and worked under assumed names. They were guilty as charged. Most in later years, when being a member of the Communist Party was made legal, publicly admitted they were guilty, would side with the Soviet Union in case of war or apologized for their indiscretions.

Alvah Bessie

Novelist and journalist, wrote screenplays for Warner Bothers; was a soldier in the Spanish Civil War in 1938 in the International Brigade. Was nominated for an Academy Award for Warner's film *Objective Burma* (1945). Ruined by the blacklisting in 1947. Never returned to Hollywood.

Herbert J. Biberman and wife Dale Sondergaard

Screenwriter and producer, blacklisted in 1950. Accused by Budd Schulberg and Edward Dymtryk of being a member of the Communist Party along with wife Dale Sondergaard. Both refused to testify. Best known in Europe and France. His last film *Slaves* (1969) was an adaptation of *Uncle Tom's Cabin*.

Lester Cole

A high school dropout at age 16, later worked as an actor on stage before embarking on a screen writing career. While in Hollywood was a union activist and co-founder of Screen Writers Guild. In 1933, was blackballed for challenging the committee's right to interrogate him about his political beliefs. When he went to jail he left behind an unfinished script to be later finished by John Steinbeck, *Viva Zapata*, (1952). He collaborated on screenplays under an assumed name and taught screenwriting at the University of California, Berkeley.

Edward Dmytrk

Editor and director at Paramount, accused of having ties with the Communist Party in 1948, sentenced for a year in prison. Upon return from prison, he went before the HUAC again as a "friendly witness" and his name was dropped from the blacklist. He resumed his career and directed for producer, Stanley Kramer, notably *The Sniper* (1952), *Caine Mutiny* (1954), *Broken Lance*, (1954), *Warlock* (1954), The *Young Lions* (1958), and about 50 less notable films.

Ring Lardner, Jr.

A publicist for David Selznick, worked uncredited as a script doctor, and full-fledged screenwriter, shared an Oscar in 1942 for *Woman of the Year*. A promising career was interrupted when he refused to testify before the HUAC and spent a year in prison and blacklisted. in 1960. While officially banned from Hollywood he worked under pseudonyms and uncredited. He made a big comeback in 1970 when he wrote the scripts for *M*A* S*H*. He wrote or collaborated on over 40 films.

John Howard Lawson

Was a volunteer ambulance driver for the Red Cross in WWI with Ernest Hemingway. After the war, began editing a newspaper in Rome. In the 20s and 30s wrote numerous plays promoting Marxism. Sold his first play to Paramount then moved to Hollywood to become a contract writer for screenplays, stories and scripts for several films. Became a co-founder of Screen Writers Guild and served as its first president. Many of Lawson's films embraced socialistic concepts. Was one of the most notorious of the Hollywood Ten. He exiled himself to Mexico where he wrote books on drama and film making.

Albert Maltz

Author, playwright and screenwriter Maltz was among the first blackballed by the HUAC for refusing to talk about communist affiliations. Following education at Columbia University and Yale School of Drama, Maltz worked as playwright for the leftist Theater Union with his plays produced in New York. He moved to Hollywood to write screenplays in 1941 working alone or in collaboration with Warner Brothers and Paramount. During WWII he wrote patriotic scripts for such films as *Destination Tokyo,* (1944))and *Moscow Strikes Back(*1942). After refusing to cooperate he was sentenced to nearly a year in jail and blacklisted.

Samuel Ornitz

Turned his back on the capitalist system where his family were prosperous retail merchants, making his first socialistic public speech at the age of 12. Though he wrote about Jewish immigrant life, his chief claim to fame in Hollywood was as an early organizer of the Screen Actors Guild, and as one of the most outspoken of Hollywood's left wing community. He served a year in prison for contempt of Congress, during which time he published *Bride of the Sabbath.* He continued writing novels until his death at age 66.

Adrian Scott

Screen writer/producer Adrian Scott was among the first ten Hollywood people to be called before the HUAC committee in the early 50s, turned in by director/producer Edward Dmytrk, with whom Scott had worked for many years. Refusing to testify, he was sentenced for a year in prison. He was blacklisted and never worked in films again.

Dalton Trumbo

Beginning his professional life as a newspaper reporter and editor, he was drawn to the movie business in the mid 30s. His most important scripts included *Five Came Back* (1939) and *Kitty Foyle* (1940) and with the outbreak of WWII wrote such classics as *A Guy Named Joe* (1943) and *Thirty Seconds Over Tokyo* (1944). His fortunes changed when he was called to testify about the communist infiltration of the movie business and along with nine others refused to testify. Was cited for contempt of Congress and sentenced to ten months in jail. Unemployable in Hollywood he moved to Mexico and continued to write under assumed names. His script for *The Brave One* (1956) under the name Robert Rich won the Academy Award. By the end of the 60s with a new generation of communist friendly executives in charge of the studios, Trumbo was welcomed back like a hero from the war, and was allowed to make a screen adaptation of the antiwar novel *Johnny Got His Gun*.(1971). It got huge press in the United States due to its relevance to the Vietnam War. Critics say the accolades were really intended to compensate him for past injustice rather than the merit of the film.

CHAPTER SIX

The Radical Left in the United States

When WWII was over, our ally in the war the Soviet Union, resumed its quest for world domination reverting to traditional Marxism. Stalin's plan for Communist expansion included:

- the creation of pro-communist puppet governments in the occupied territories,
- military conquest of new territories by satellite armies (not their own) and
- infiltration of free countries by Soviet spy and propaganda organizations.

In the Free World there were three interpretations of communist policy and three different recommendations as to how best to deal with the communist threat.

The first group accepted the communists as the world revolutionists they professed to be and assumed their past behavior was the safest indication of how they could be expected to act in the future.

The second group took a more idealistic view, preferring to look upon communist behavior as political immaturity which could be changed by patient endurance and generosity on our side.[20]

The third group accepted the communists as revolutionists, but didn't believe they could take over the world, and simply re-acted diplomatically with the reasoning that a Cold War was better than a shooting war.

President Franklin Roosevelt seemed to take the second view. When past U. S. Ambassador to Russia, William C. Bullitt, warned the President to keep up his guard in dealing with the communist leaders, he was reported in Life Magazine, August 30, 1948, P 94 as saying, "Bill, I don't dispute your facts; they are accurate. I don't dispute the logic of your reasoning. I just have a hunch that Stalin is not that kind of man.

"Harry (Hopkins) says he is not, and that he doesn't want anything but security for his country. And I think that if I give him everything that I can, and ask him for nothing in return…he won't try to annex anything and will work with me for a world of peace and democracy." [21]

Previously at the Dunbarton Oaks conference in Washington D.C. representatives of Britain, China, Russia and the United States had met to lay the constitutional foundation for the United Nations where Russia was made a full and dominant partner. Russia insisted on the veto power even if she was partner to the dispute. The democracies objected but consented. They were ready to bend over backwards, pay any price, for Russian participation.

A few months later the Prime Minister of England was becoming fed up and urged Roosevelt that a "blunt and firm stand should be made in our countries in order to clear the air and make Russia realize there is a point beyond which we will not tolerate insult."

There is some indication that President Roosevelt was beginning to awaken to reality but died before he could answer the message.

The task of building the UN fell into the hands of those who still insisted that the Russians were being misunderstood. A State Department employee, Alger Hiss, would chair the International Assembly.

The Charter of the United Nations is remarkably similar to the Communist Constitution of Russia which is characterized by declaration of democratic principles followed by procedural limitations that nullified the principles just announced. In the same fashion the UN Charter provides for the sovereign equality of all its members and then sets up a Security Council which is dominated by five members (U.S. Britain. Russia. China and France) anyone of which can nullify the desires of all other member nations by exercise of the veto power.

We had established a world-wide police organization and made the top international gangster a member with veto power of any sanctions against his actions. Peace-loving nations were in for a violent and stormy era as a result of the strategy of making the Soviets full partners of the free world.

The China Debacle

The U.S. diplomats who had helped to set up the United Nations, and who insisted that the "peaceful" communist leaders were "agrarian reformers" and had no territorial ambitions, denounced Chiang Kai-shek, leader of the Chinese Nationalists who was preparing China for a constitutional form of government, as the real problem in China. They sent General George C. Marshall over to stop the civil war between the Communists and Nationalists, which the Nationalists was winning.

Three different times they ordered Chiang to issue an unconditional cease fire. When he refused, United States aid was terminated. While the Nationalists were being held down by U.S. diplomatic pressure, the communists counter-attacked. The U.S. embargo was not lifted until too late, and China became a part of the communist world.[22] There was a storm of indignation in the United States, but the men who engineered the communist takeover collaborated on a report to justify their action. Their White Paper called "United States Relations with China," proved the diplomatic strategists were not willing to change their evaluation of communist leaders, though the evidence of duplicity was everywhere.[23]

The Debacle of South Korea

Secretary of State Dean Acheson overruled the Joint Chiefs of Staff who wanted to give strong military aid to Chiang by announcing on January 12, 1950 that the Chinese Communists should be allowed to take over Formosa, now Taiwan, where Chiang was in exile, and that no aid should be given the anti-communist guerrillas in South China.[24]

He announced further that the U. S. defense perimeter did not include either Formosa or South Korea. This invited communist attack on these allies by giving advance notice that these areas could be invaded without interference from the United States. (The freedom to invade Formosa was removed by the UN when the UN gave communist China the Nationalist's UN seat with the proviso that they would leave Formosa alone.)

Six months later the communists attacked South Korea. It should be noted that the Yalta agreement had allowed Russia to take over North Korea at the same time the Soviets occupied Manchuria.

A spokesman for the U.S. diplomats, Owen Lattimore said, "The thing to do is let South Korea fall and not let it look as though we pushed it."[25]

The Security Council of the UN ruled that North Korea was guilty of a breach of peace and ordered them back to the 38th parallel. President Truman completely reversed the policy of his military advisors and ordered General Douglas MacArthur who was made Supreme Commander of UN forces, to pour U.S. troops in from Japan.

MacArthur through brilliant tactics and a daring landing at Inchon trapped the North Koreans and cut their supply lines. He turned his armies to the north. By mid-October the UN offensive was near the northern border of Korea, and the war appeared to be nearly over.

Then disaster struck. A Chinese Communist army of a million men swarmed over the border and pushed the UN troops below the 38th parallel. MacArthur could not believe that the Chinese Communists would risk the massive retaliation of the United States by the inexcusable attack on UN Forces.

What he did not know until later was that the Chinese had already been assured by their intelligence agents that the diplomats in Washington, were not going to allow MacArthur to retaliate as he was being restricted to "limited" warfare.[26] It was then that MacArthur became aware that pro-communist forces in the UN and left wing sympathizers in the State Department were swamping the policies of the White House, Joint Chiefs of Staff and those in charge of the Korean War.[27]

The diplomats had imposed upon our military a theory originated by George Kennan called "Communist Containment" which actually resulted in the containment of UN fighting forces instead of the communists. It soon became apparent that the Korean War was being run by the same team and according to the same policies which resulted in the fall of China.[28]

Among other things MacArthur was specifically forbidden from following Chinese jets to their bases, or bombing the Manchurian

Railroad or the Yalu River bridge which was a major enemy supply route for troops and supplies. His own supplies and replacements were cut back; to the point where a counter-attack was just about impossible.

On December 6, 1950 General MacArthur violated a presidential gag order by answering a written inquiry from Congressman Joseph Martin and giving his recommendations for winning the war. President Truman ordered General MacArthur withdrawn from all commands.

The United States Debacle

The communist strategy for the United States was to appeal to the idealistic group who did not see the bear or understand the communist menace, with the objective always to soften up the target, divide and conquer. The tactics were psychological. Infiltrate the country, send in underground agents, or recruit moles already here (American citizens), with the idea of placing them in high level posts come the revolution. The moles and agents spoke our local language fluently and were part of the community. The moles, who would be underground and their status not known to anybody, even their family, were named for those furry little animals that burrow just under the ground.

Our intelligence sources tell us the moles were instructed to infiltrate the government at all levels, academia, communications apparatus such as print, radio, television and movies, churches, big business and even the military, keep a low profile, and move into responsible positions. It was a "It may be 15–20 years before we need you, but you be ready when we do," kind of a thing.

This cohesive group, including many academicians, clearly opposed our Cold War stance, retained some degree of sympathy for both the Soviet Union and for Marxism, and influenced thousands of students to their view. Even today many university professors in this country see Karl Marx only as an economist and teach his theory as a viable alternative to capitalism. Look in any college curriculum program.

Radical Left students, by and large, viewed religion as useful insofar as the churches helped further the goal of building a heaven on earth (humane Marxism, if you will) under New Left auspices.[29]

The student's fathers were mostly wealthy, well educated, upper middle class professionals such as college faculty, doctors and lawyers. Their parents were politically liberal and shared the socially liberal values of estheticism, secularism and self expression.[30]

(I hate big words because they slow a reader down and interrupt the rhythm of the language. Simply stated this means they are showoffs, agnostics, and if perchance there is a God, it is they. Not very nice people.)

Educationally there were a high percentage of graduate students and teaching assistants in political science, history, economics and philosophy. They were apt to be found in liberal institutions such as the University of California at Berkeley, University of Michigan, Columbia University, University of Wisconsin and Ivy League schools (such as Harvard and Yale).[31]

After the big war, the radical left put on a full-court press to recruit moles, dupes, party members and fellow travelers. The thousands of writers, students, labor leaders, and actors who openly joined the American Communist Party faced few legal barriers. Many held high government positions (most notably in the State Department) as the civil service did not screen on ideological grounds.[32]

A storm of protests arose as Americans realized what was happening, especially involving the loss of China and Cuba. A young Senator from Wisconsin, Joe McCarthy, was outraged and chaired Senate hearings to expose communists in government, televised so the public could see. The House Un-American Activities Committee was formed to look into the problem. A number of ex-communists in government became disenchanted and turned states evidence.

A notable case, among many, was reformed communist Whittaker Chambers who accused State Department diplomat Alger Hiss, (remember?) of passing secret documents to Soviet agents. Richard Nixon believed Chambers and was a prosecutor for the House Committee on Un-American Activities. Hiss was convicted and sent to jail for perjury.[33]

Surely Russia stole the (atomic) bomb secrets through the aid of countless communist confederates in the State Department. Some of the documents containing atomic bomb secrets which were intercepted by our military, but ordered released to Russia by Harry Hopkins, carried a note "from Hiss." Hiss started out in the Department of Agriculture, served a while in the Department of Justice, then went to the State Department, serving as Director of Political Affairs, advisor to President Roosevelt at Yalta and as Secretary-General of the International Assembly which created the United Nations.[34]

You may say that is ancient history. Not so! We are learning that the danger is not over. Steve Mills of the *Chicago Tribune*, distributed by Knight-Ridder *Tribune News Wire*, and published in *The Dallas Morning News* stated that the radical left is still very much in the picture.[35] Professors at Northwestern University and DePaul University say that the radical left is searching for new direction and focus but radicals like Jack Spiegel from Chicago still say "capitalism has to fall."

As a part of the opening of the 104th Congress on January 3, 1995, CSPAN cable television broadcasted the news conference of the House Progressive Caucus. The representatives, all Democrats, pointed out they were made up of caucus members from all the other caucuses. They chose "progressive" — a name often associated with the socialist agenda and said they planned to carry the fight to the new Republican majority.

The *Economist* magazine recently reported that opinion polls in Russia give Gennady Zyuganov, leader of the Russian Communist Party, an even chance to win the presidential election in June 1996. Russian voters, the articles said, "will do well to savor the occasion because it might be long time before they vote for a president again." He lost.

In the article titled "A dreadful prospect," the writer said that while Zyuganov is smooth and conciliatory with foreigners he gives the Russian people the hard line of a return to communism and restoration of the old Soviet Union. He and his new communist big-wigs, as mid-level zealots were spared from an overview of the hopeless struggle to stave off disaster, saw a system that worked well enough until hijacked and dismantled by Mikhail Gorbachev and may try to return to it. The writer said it is a hideous certainty that whoever wins the election it will be the wrong man. All the candidates including Boris Yeltson, Zyuganov and Gorbachev have shortcomings. Mr. Gorbacbev's aim was not to abolish communism but to modernize it and inspires gratitude for letting the Soviet Union collapse without swamping it in blood. But Russians still blame him for the chaotic aftermath of communism, and what he believes now is anybody's guess. Mr Zyuganov might well turn Russia into a troublemaker again so Mr. Yeltsin was not be counted out. He persuaded his countrymen that he was the least awful of the presidents on offer.[36]

None of us can say, with certainty, we have never been directly or indirectly responsive to the socialist agenda or communist party's influence. In President Ronald Reagan's last election campaign and before the apparent fall of communism his campaign developed a television commercial which stated "There is a bear in the woods."

Many people did not ever see that bear and do not believe he ever existed. They believe that the communists had no part in the street uprisings in the U.S. against the Vietnam War or no part in the communist propaganda that has filled our media for fifty years or more.

Thomas Sowell wrote, "One of the few things worse than being in a war is being in a war and not knowing it. The battle to break down the moral standards, the ideals and morals of this country is being waged on a thousand fronts....from the elementary schools to the universities, from Hollywood to Broadway, from the television news to the art galleries and from the courts to Congress."[37]

An Associated Press article[38] reported that after dusting off thousands of files in Moscow, American researchers say they now have proof that the Communist Party of the United States did the bidding of the Soviet spy masters. This de-bunks and agonizes the scholars who have long contended that the Communist Party USA had no spying role, that it was simply a homegrown, populist party with radical views, which in itself was exactly what the communists wanted us to believe.

Another new discovery, according to the article, was that the Communist Party USA was very much a part of the Comintem founded by Lenin in 1919 to support communist activities in other countries.

Murchison warns that the left still rules the colleges, the media and the church and doesn't want to surrender.[39]

New Left leader Sam Brown. chairman of the Americans for Democratic Action (ADA), headed up an Anti-Vietnam Moratorium Committee, which held a massive protest against the war in 1968. One of his organizers was Bill Clinton. In 1977 President Jimmy Carter would appoint Brown as director of ACTION in charge of volunteer programs such as Vista and the Peace Corps.[40] Mr. Carter would grant asylum and pardon the demonstrators who had left the country and went to Canada to avoid military service.

If I were a communist leader bent upon taking over the U.S. and in charge of recruiting moles, I think I would have taken a good look at young Mr. Clinton.

Mr. Pauken, a student at Georgetown while Mr. Clinton was there, was a national leader of the conservative students during the terrible sixties who had debated the radical leftists on numerous occasions and knew their leaders well. After his tour in Vietnam, he was appointed aide to John Dean, legal counsel to President Richard Nixon. He said that one problem for the President during this period was that almost all of his young staff were strongly opposed to our involvement in the Vietnam War and sided with the New Left view that we were supporting the wrong side.

Pauken's assessment is that the anti-war leftist movement was the most serious internal security threat since the communist mass movements in the 30s and the Soviet spy rings and front groups in the 40s and 50s. Older and wiser, the sixties radicals are much better positioned now to undermine the system they learned to hate long ago. A French Jesuit at Georgetown University proclaimed that a perfect world (heaven on earth) is within our potential. The progressive priests in charge of the school turned the place upside down almost overnight in their rush to embrace this (Marxist-Leninist) vision of utopia.[41]

We are now deeply involved in the War on Terrorism, but Liberal professors still hate capitalism and tend to reject conservative arguments as not being worthy of serious discussion.[42] Parents with college students would do well to look into what their children are being taught. This generation of students are being required to shoulder the defense of freedom from an enemy which grew up on hate and a full dose of brute force and violence.

If anything the Radical Left is larger and stronger now than in the 60s and 70s. The enemy is on the ground in America and has declared the war on America to be a Holy War involving virtually every Muslim in the world.

Tough mindedness and reality thinking might be in order.

CHAPTER SEVEN

The Problem Our Courts Face

*Human ingenuity has never been able to devise a system of
guaranteeing freedom for the wise and honest except by
guaranteeing freedom for all; and freedom for the wise is so
supremely important that is worth the price of making the silly
free, too.*
— Gerald W. Johnson[43]

Johnson's statement expresses a point of view most Americans
cherish. Within this spirit a great many anti-communists have
opposed all attempts to distinguish between communists and non-
communists in terms of freedoms to be exercised. How would it
sound if we added the words "including the conspiratorial" after
"freedom for all?" Not so good. Can we find a way, consistent with
liberty under law, of protecting ourselves against the communist
conspiracy while also preserving our freedoms?

Admittedly I have been harshly critical of the position our courts
have taken in giving aid and comfort to the communists who were
using our freedoms to destroy us.

We held no brief for the Nazis during WWII, yet we have time
and again managed to put Soviet agents in a different category. By
articles written and speeches made in support of them, Soviet agents
are shown as victims. "If this poor fellow can be victimized any of us
can be framed on trumped up charges."

A communist pamphlet titled "Under Arrest! How to Defend
Yourself in Court! What to do When Arrested and Questioned!"
distributed on a mass basis by the Labor Defender, New York City,
at five cents a copy gives us an example of what the courts are up
against.[44]

The pamphlet states, "The class struggle goes on in the courtroom
as it does on the picket line, in the shops and in the mines."

81

It contains more than thirty five pages on how to stall legal procedures, create confusion in the courtroom, plant strategic doubts in the public mind, put forth the Marxist-Leninist concept of law, prove the class bias of the court by statements which can only be disproved by long digressions, and demand every right and safeguard provided by the law of the land.

Further the party member is told to make the courtroom his forum by bringing out class issues at the trial, exposing the method of selecting jury panels, making a demand for a new panel, and when the judge denies the challenge showing that the court stands as a capitalist tool for the suppression of the working class and taking advantage of every opportunity to state that the workers expect no justice in a capitalist court.

The judges, when they have to handle a case involving communists, are thus up against an organized conspiracy to obstruct legal procedures and destroy public confidence in these procedures.

This legal debris left over from the Cold War was seen in stark reality in the O. J. Simpson trial when the defense stalled procedures for over a year, created confusion in the courtroom, made the murder case a race issue, and successfully showed that our courts are racist, and that an African-American person could never get a fair trial and could actually be framed by the system.

This is not to accuse anyone connected with the case of any communist leanings, but our democratic legal system has learned some tactics from the Cold War and is on thin ice. I was horrified to hear an ex-Harvard law professor on 60 Minutes advocate and exhort black juries to declare not guilty and release any black defendant whose crime did not involve murder.

But, as long as litigants and defendants hold fast to these strategies and tactics which set class-against-class, it should be outside the law, whether or not it is declared illegal.[45]

The Preamble to the Constitution which we regard as the Supreme Law of the land begins:

"We the people of the United States, in order to form a more perfect Union, establish justice, provide for the common defense, promote the general welfare and secure the blessings of liberty for ourselves and our posterity..."

Clearly our Founding Fathers considered the Constitution to be a document for the harmonizing of disagreements and differences and for the affirmation of common stakes; not for the arbitrary dividing of mankind into warring classes.

CHAPTER EIGHT

Common Sense

One man, Thomas Paine, may have had more influence on America's Founding Fathers than any other. You remember, "These are the times that try men's souls." That was Thomas Paine. He was a young writer, a British subject only two years in America, not well known in American circles, and not a member of any American deliberating panels. Others would be given credit for the Declaration of Independence and the form of our new Constitution and government, yet his ideas were followed almost to the letter.

Early on before the Revolutionary War, Paine wrote a series of articles first published in January 1776 called "Common Sense." This was the time when we had just about had it with England and their Stamp Act, occupying troops, and customs laws, and taxation without representation. In 1773 some Massachusetts patriots had dressed themselves like Indians and dumped crates of tea into Boston Harbor to protest the British Tea Act. The Minute Men had fired on British troops at Lexington and Concord in April 1775, the "shots heard around the world," and forced them back to Boston.

On July 4, 1776, Congress ratified Thomas Jefferson's Declaration of Independence, which Paine had suggested six months before. Within the month a huge British force landed in New York harbor to try and crush the revolution. The war was just starting with a shoe-string army with George Washington in charge.

Got the time straight? OK. "These are the times to try men's souls," wrote Paine and prophesied that we couldn't expect much from the summer soldiers and sunshine patriots. We don't. He wrote it was inevitable that sooner or later a split was bound to occur between England and America. A super power, situated on an island

5,000 miles away, could not adequately govern, or control, a growing continent of spirited men and women, who valued their liberty so much they brought their families into God-knows-what dangers to escape the tyranny of kings.

Paine thought that "Small islands incapable of defending themselves may be the proper object for Kings to take under their care, but it is absurd to suppose that a continent should be perpetually governed by an island."

He wrote, "The sun never shined on a cause of greater worth." Volumes had been written on the subject of the struggle between England and America, but now the debate was closed after the shots heard around the world Minute Man episode. "We have come to blows," wrote King George III. "By referring the matter from argument to arms," Paine wrote, "a new era for politics is struck, a new method of thinking" is required. All plans and proposals prior to April 19, 1775, are like last year's almanacs, maybe all right then, but of no use now.

There were many who did not agree with the Revolution and wanted to make peace with England. Paine wrote that while he wanted to avoid giving unnecessary offense, those who espouse the doctrine of reconciliation with England either were:

- Men who had a vested interest and could not be trusted,
- Weak men who cannot see,
- Prejudiced men who will not see, and
- Moderate men who think more of the European world than it deserves.

This last group, he said, by ill-judged deliberation will be the cause of more calamities to this continent than all the other three. We would see the same thing played out in the Cold War and the War against Terrorism.

Paine's greatest contribution was in four areas:

- Declaring "the time is NOW" to strike out for Liberty
- No King in the new Republic.
- House of Representatives and Senate, and how it would be formed.
- How to go about gaining the support of the rest of the world.

All of Paine's arguments, with minor modifications, were accepted by the Continental Convention in September, 1787. The "Common

Sense" articles had been debated, discussed, and argued about for 11 years before the Convention that finally would decide what our Constitution would be like.

What does this have to do with us 228 years later? Follow me. There is a point here. There is a huge debate going on now in this country about the state of mind of our Founding Fathers when they formed the Constitution. What did their words mean? The Supreme Court bases its opinions on that interpretation. Since Paine was their consultant as it were, the engineer who built a path they would follow, knowing his logic, which the Founders debated over a number of years and accepted, we can pretty much know what they were thinking. Is that Common Sense? I think so.

Now Is the Time to Strike the Blow for Liberty

It is not in the power of Britain or of Europe to conquer America if she does not conquer herself by delay and timidity, Paine wrote. While he had no sympathy for those who sought a reconciliation with England, he was concerned about the citizenry of Boston who were captured by the British (endangered by the fire of their friends if they stayed in the city, but plundered by the British if they tried to leave). They were prisoners without hope of redemption. In any attack by the Americans for their relief, they would be exposed to the fury of both armies.

"I challenge the warmest advocate for reconciliation to show a single advantage this continent can reap, by being connected with Great Britain. Our corn will fetch its price in any market in Europe, and our imported goods must be paid for, buy them where we will." However, the injuries and disadvantages are without number. Europe has too many kingdoms to be long at peace. Whenever a war breaks out between England and any foreign power, the trade of America goes to ruin because of her connection with England.

He wrote that the distance the Almighty has placed between England and America is strong and natural proof that the authority of one over the other was never the design of Heaven. America's discovery before the reformation was as if the Almighty graciously meant to open a sanctuary to the persecuted in future years when home could afford neither friendship nor safety.

The time is NOW. "Tis time to part...as Britain has not shown the slightest inclination towards a compromise, in spite of an appeal from the Continental Congress, we can be assured no terms equal to the blood, expense and treasure we have already been put to," he said.

Doing otherwise than continuing the fight for Liberty would be the ruin of the continent. The governing powers will still be in the hand of the king who will have a negative over the whole legislation of the continent. He is not a proper man to say to these colonies, "You shall make no laws but what I please." The king's negative here is ten times more dangerous here than in England. He can scarcely refuse his consent for putting England into as strong a state of defense as possible, but in America he would never allow such a bill to be passed.

"A government that cannot preserve our peace, is no government at all, and in that case we pay our money for nothing," Paine wrote.

The Declaration of Independence

Paine wrote, it is the custom of nations, when any two are at war, for some other powers not engaged in the quarrel to step in as mediators. America was still calling herself the subject of Great Britain, so no other power could offer to mediate. We could not expect the other great powers, France and Spain, to give any kind of assistance because they would be sufferers by the consequences. While professing ourselves the subjects of Great Britain, in the eyes of foreign nations, we were rebels. They could be drawn into the war.

Six months before it was written, Paine suggested a declaration of our independence to clear the air with other countries as to our intentions. His words: "Were a manifesto to be published, and dispatched to foreign courts, setting forth the miseries we have endured, and the peaceful methods we have ineffectually used for redress; declaring at the same time, that not being able, any longer, to live happily or safely under the cruel disposition of the British court, we had been driven to the necessity of breaking off all connections with her; at the same time assuring all such courts of our peaceful disposition towards them, and of our desire to enter into trade with them: Such a declaration would produce more good effects to this continent, than if a ship were freighted with petitions to Britain."

Under the situation as British subjects, America could not be received nor heard abroad, until by declaring our independence, we take rank with the other nations. Only common sense. The Continental Congress took the suggestion and appointed a committee. Thomas Jefferson did the writing.

No King for America...the Lord Reigns Above

There has been a great deal of argument lately in America in support of separation of church and state, and that no religious activity such as prayers in school or even Christmas decorations on federal property should be allowed.

Here is what Paine had to say, slightly edited for brevity: *"Where, some ask, is the King of America? I'll tell you, Friend, he reigns above.* Let a day be solemnly set aside for proclaiming the charter; let it be brought forth placed *on the divine law, the word of God;* let a (symbolic) crown be placed thereon, by which the world may know, that in America the (divine) Law is King. In absolute governments the King is Law, so in free countries the Law ought to be King, and there ought to be no other."

Since Paine's words and arguments were picked up and used in our Constitution, Bill of Rights, Declaration of Independence and the form of our governmental bodies, i.e., President, Congress, and the Legal system, and the word "God" is inserted on almost every page in almost every document, it is common sense to me our Founding Fathers intended this to be one nation, under God.

It seems clear to me that our forefathers intended God to be an integral part of our system of government, *like any other of its parts*, and keenly aware that since all the other republics the world has known have not lasted, *this should be the glue* that would hold our republic together. When asked after the Constitutional Convention what "they had brought us," Benjamin Franklin said, "A Republic, if you can keep it."

As to religion Paine wrote, "For myself, I fully and conscientiously believe that it is the will of the Almighty, that there should be a diversity of religious opinions among us. It affords a larger field for our Christian kindness. On this principle, I look on the various denominations among us to be like children of the same family."

It is interesting that after the Continental Congress, colonial Connecticut set up a state religion but abandoned it in 1787 after the Constitution was ratified.

Our King Let Us Down in the Cold War

Thomas Paine's vision of the Law as King came to pass in America. If the Law is King, then our Supreme Court is King. A majority of the Court, five people, who almost no person in America knows by name, says to you and me, "There shall be no laws but those we like." So long as the Court is manned by good and able men and women, who stick by the Constitution and the laws of morality and justice and who don't make up the law as they go along, the King is good. Presidents often appoint judges on the basis of political expediency, or political correctness, sometimes meeting them for the first time after the appointment. Senate confirmation hearings televised to the public often causes one to wonder, "Is that the best we have to be our King?"

Like other monarchs the judges sometimes stay in their chambers, lose touch with what is going on out there, abandon moral absolutes set there to guide them, and make their judgments according to their own vision of what America should be. Unfortunately, that was what we have had on the bench since WWII. One of their prime responsibilities is the protection of our people, securing our property and freedom, and the free exercise of religion, according to the dictates of our conscience.

These monarchs somehow missed that the Communist Party USA and militant Islam conspirators are not just political parties in America, and they opened the doors to free use of all our institutions, with no rules to restrict their behavior. Either they are blind, were conspirators, or helpless against the lawyers. Freedom has become license, with the criminal protected and the victim exposed, clearly **not** what the Founding Fathers had in mind or would countenance now.

We learned in my civics class in the 40s about justice under the law. Now any lawyer will tell you there is no justice. There is only the law. What is the law? It is what the judges say it is, which often brings down judgments so ludicrous they are unbelievable. We have laws against spitting on sidewalks and not picking up after our dogs, but no law against burning the flag, the symbol of Liberty. Standing up in classrooms, teaching the overthrow of our country, or rioting in the streets with associated looting and pillaging is protected as freedom of speech by our King, the Supreme Court of our land. That defies common sense.

I could go on and on, but you get, and probably share my concerns about what has happened to America in the last fifty years. We have become a nation of nit-pickers and whiners with no idea of the damage we are doing to ourselves and others, while the lawyers are picking our collective bones. Our laws are so complicated and numerous that our legal house resembles a large clapboard barn with boards nailed every which direction. Nobody knows all the laws, so lawyers can sue anybody on any charge and have a good chance of winning.

The law is what our King, the Supreme Court, wants it to be. If we are to recover from this national illness, we have some work to do. We must first examine and remove the laws that permit an outside enemy, bent on conquering us, free access to our freedoms.

Paine said over 225 years ago that some ideologue may hereafter arise and by laying hold of popular disquietudes, collect together the desperate and discontented, and by assuming the powers of government sweep away the liberties of the continent like a deluge. "Ere you hear the news the fatal business might be done," he said, "leaving ourselves suffering under the oppression of a conqueror."

The communists thought their time would be in 1973. In 1972 we had a candidate for President of the Unites States join rioters in the street in America, cheer for a foreign enemy, and actually visit the enemy in wartime, action that would have been treason, punishable by death in any other age, all under the protection of the Supreme Court. That defies Common Sense. Only Divine Providence has kept us from losing it all.

Paine concluded his "Common Sense" essay thusly:

"Oh ye that love mankind! Ye that dare oppose, not only the tyranny but the tyrant, stand forth. Every spot in the old world is overrun with oppression. Freedom is hunted around the globe. Asia and Africa hath long expelled her. Europe regards her like a stranger. Oh, receive the fugitive and prepare an asylum for mankind "

The "asylum for mankind" that they prepared is America, and we are a Republic living on borrowed time. In World War II there were signs everywhere reminding citizens and soldiers alike that, "United We Stand, Divided We Fall."

Today that sign reads "United We Fall, Divided We Stand." We are being persuaded that it is our duty to hate America, hate our government, hate our President, and encourage those who would do America harm. Thomas Paine, our Founding Fathers, and the dead of all our wars are rolling in their graves. The end of that road promises death for America.

With apologies to Thomas Paine, "It is not in the power of Communism or Islam or the Terrorists to conquer America, if she does not conquer herself by blindness, procrastination or timidity."

I believe it was George Bush, the elder, who said, "America would not be the land of the free, if she was not also the home of the brave."

CHAPTER NINE

Conclusion and Recommendations

"Mankind has known but a few moments of Freedom in its entire history. Most of these moments have been ours. All of them have come under a system of free enterprise."
— President Ronald Reagan

We have been a free nation for 228 years as of July 4, 2004, moments old as history goes. To put that in perspective, most WWII servicemen, and that includes me, have been alive a third of that time.

We have been in at least ten wars in those 228 years. Just about every generation of Americans has had its war. At this moment there are between 150-200 armed conflicts going on around the globe. Probably there has been no time in man's recorded history when there has been no war. Nations are born and nations die.

We don't know what form our next war will take. We can only extrapolate that there will be one and another and another. Hopefully we can learn so that there will never be another like the Cold War where our freedoms were used as a weapon against us.

Life Stages of a Civilization

There are at least ten identifiable stages in the life of every major civilization in history.[46] The average age of a civilization is a little over 200 years, so many years may pass in each stage. Our problems would exist if there were no radical left menace.

Bondage – Citizens fall under bondage from an invader or dictator. This may be external or internal as happened in Nazi Germany and the Soviet Union.

Spiritual faith – Citizens pray to their God for strength to endure and for delivery from bondage.

Great Courage – People rise up and throw off the chains of slavery and dictatorship. Patrick Henry put his life on the line when he stood in the House of Burgesses in Williamsburg, Virginia, and shouted the words, "I know not what course others may take, but as for me, give me liberty or give me death." The Founding Fathers did likewise.

Freedom – Citizens feel a new energy, breathe the fresh air of freedom and work hard to harvest the comforts and opportunities of life. They help each other to "build the barns." Iraq is finding that bondage and dependency were easy to learn. Freedom, democracy and self-reliance take a little longer.

Abundance – Every one who wants a job has one. Everyone is well fed, well clothed and sheltered. Life is great. No help needed.

Selfishness – People begin to notice that some are living better and begin to covet their neighbors' possessions and hold on tight to theirs. "What's in it for me?" becomes the national cry.

Complacency – Many people settle back with a defeatist attitude. "There's no way to win anymore. Might as well get by with what we have."

Apathy – A "Let George do it" attitude prevails. People stay away from the polls as "elected officials do what they want to anyway." "There are no jobs out there so I will wait until something comes along." Apathetic Societies form — if you want to join, you are not eligible.

Dependency – People begin to turn to government for everything. Huge debt burdens the government and it falls bankrupt.

Bondage – A strong man arises or an invading enemy takes over, and the cycle starts all over again. The public does not resist until it is too late.

— First author unknown.

Our experiment with democracy, freedom for all, and the republican form of government is an infant as history goes. We are in the end stages of the cycle, and there are no guarantees that we will be here forever. Can we turn back the clock and short circuit the cycle? Some say no. I am more optimistic.

Ten Suggestions That Will Make America Better

I would like to offer Ten Suggestions as to how each of us, working together, might have a happier life, make America a better place, and short circuit the cycle by changing our behavior. Behavior must change first, then attitudes change, not the other way around.

1. Loosen up. The Ten Commandments are a part of every religion in one form or another. It is a good plan for living a happy and prosperous life. I wouldn't mind my grandchildren learning these universal principles in school. If you went to kindergarten you learned most of them. School is a very good place for learning discipline, courtesy and moral responsibility toward others. Moral responsibility means, "I will do my best to do my duty, because I pledge to do it, and I keep my word."

2. Learn to honor the flag and salute it every chance you get. If you don't have a flagpole at home, get one and fly the flag. Learn to fold it and fly it properly. Treat it like the precious symbol of your freedom that it is.

3. Learn the national anthem and sing it every chance you get. Think about the words and what they mean. Learn the words to other patriotic songs. Sing them often, out loud and proudly, if only in the shower. Keep a song in your heart for America.

4. Learn the Pledge of Allegiance to the flag and participate every time you have the opportunity. Say it out loud and proudly and mean it. Your pledge is your word and your honor is at stake.

5. Get a copy or recording of General Douglas MacArthur's **"Duty, Honor, Country"** speech to the cadets at West Point. Listen to every word.

6. Appreciate America more. On your travels abroad think about what it would be like living in the countries you visit.

7. Love your country. When somebody trashes it, set them straight. The United States is not perfect — after all we are only 228 years old — but we are better than anything else out there. We can, and expect to, be better. We are getting there. Don't give up on America.

8. Get on the team. Serve your country in any way that you can. As a military retiree I feel that every citizen owes his country a hitch in the military or service of some kind. I gave 20 years — some gave their lives. I still feel indebted. Your country doesn't owe you anything. You owe it everything. You will learn many lessons that will serve you well in private life.

9. Participate in Memorial services to commemorate the sacrifices others have made for your freedom. Somehow I think they will know that you did — and you will feel great.

10. Develop a good attitude and a sense of personal honor by minding your behavior. Be courteous in all that you do. Remember your freedom ends where the other fellow's nose begins.

Happiness is self-centered and fleeting — the Joy of Living lasts a lifetime and comes with service to others — of what you invest in them and they invest in you.

America needs you! Be there!

APPENDIX A

Crisis Averted at Berkeley

Early in May, 1970 I received a form letter with enclosure from A.M. Hopkin, Chairman of the Department of Engineering and Computer Sciences, University of California, Berkeley, California, in my capacity as chief human resources executive of a major Texas corporation.

It gave me a chilling feeling to realize what was happening on American college campuses, up-close and personal, and how close we came to losing it all.

This epistle was apparently sent out as a large general mailing because we had never recruited at Berkeley. His purpose became clear when he asked me to participate in the students' and professors' protest action by expressing my support to the lawmakers of this country and to others in positions of power and influence, to stop the war in Indochina and to express concern over the constitutional questions in the widening of the Indochina war.

The action they were taking was to close the school of engineering, professors and students together, to end a war "which constitutes a threat not only for the peoples of Indochina but for the whole of mankind," and along with other universities prepare for a national strike, and to refuse to resume normal activities in the Fall if the war was not stopped by that time.

It is chilling to think what would have happened if their proposed action had picked up support and there had been a national college strike? Can you believe that a handful of American radicals, acting in support of a communist cause, could accomplish this? What would American parents and lawmakers have done? Would they have caved?

This was too much for me, as I was sure I knew infinitely more about the war than they did, as clearly all they had was the communist propaganda view. So I fired him a letter.

Why did I have to do that? Where was our media which should have been balancing the communist propaganda with the true communist story? We wouldn't have had the problem if the media had reported the facts and stayed out of the propaganda game.

Apparently my letter hit a nerve, because he wrote back a personal letter stating that he had made my letter available to the students, so "they may better realize their problem in communicating their concerns" to blockheads like me.

He announced incidentally that both the students and the professors had reconsidered, and they were not going to close the school after all. He expressed his and the faculty's concern that the students not go "the radical way," a course he and thirty seven other faculty members were ready to take less than a month before.

Did my letter stop the professors and students at Berkeley? I doubt it, but it would be nice to think it brought a flicker of a candle's light of reason to the UC Berkeley School of Engineering and Computer Science. It does make me believe that most Americans, in the company of the facts, will not do something that will harm their country.

The handwriting at the end of the professor's last letter reads as follows:

"In looking over this letter I realize that there is a discrepancy between it and the original letter which is based on the time elapsed between. In the meantime our faculty have kept open their classes and have encouraged students to seek responsible action as an outlet for their emotions, have scheduled make-up sections and have brought students back to their technical education efforts. What we feel we have to lose is that many, many young people may go radical — a process from which it is hard to return, and for which we *all* pay a great price. Our strong concern is that our students remain engineers and that they not go the radical way." A. M. Hopkin

Bravo, professor! But you still didn't seem to have a clue as to what or who was making students go radical and for what purpose. Let us hope that you, and people like you, may be smarter a quarter of a century later.

ROBERT E. WILLIAMS

Dept.of Electrical Engineering
 and Computer Sciences
University of California
Berkeley, California 94720

May 8, 1970

Dear Sir:

As a recruiter, you will be concerned with recent disturbances on the campuses of universities across the country. The recent U. S. invasion of Cambodia has created an extremely disruptive situation in the Electrical Engineering department at Berkeley. In the several preceeding campus crises, electrical engineering students, by and large, did not participate or participated in token form only, and for the most part continued to attend their technical classes. In this present emergency, a large number of our students have pledged to cease attending classes for the remainder of the quarter, to use the Summer to prepare for a national strike and to refuse to resume their normal activities in the fall if the war has not stopped by that time. By and large, students in our department are not 'radicals', but have the reputation of being one of the most conservative groups on campus. Our students are so very deeply troubled by the continuing war in Indochina, however, that they refuse to study or attend classes.

Many of us on the faculty of the Electrical Engineering department find ourselves in agreement with the aims of the students. The Electrical Engineering faculty has strongly endorsed the enclosed statement. We hope you will bring it to the attention of your colleagues.

Sincerely,
A. M. Hopkin
Chairman
AMH:ps
Enclosure

HAS AMERICA LOST HER WAY?

THE UNDERSIGNED FACULTY MEMBERS OF THE ELECTRICAL ENGINEERING DEPARTMENT OF THE UNIVERSITY OF CALIFORNIA, BERKELEY are deeply troubled over recent events in Indochina.

In the present emergency, a large number of University of California students have pledged to cease attending classes for the remainder of the quarter, to use the Summer to prepare for a national strike, and to refuse to resume their normal activities in the Fall if the war has not stopped by that time.

Many of our electrical engineering faculty are joining with faculty and students in universities across the country in suspending their normal activities in order to communicate to our government and the people outside the university community our concern over the widening of the Indochina war, and the constitutional questions raised by our President's recent actions. We urge you to participate by expressing your opinion to the lawmakers of this country, and to others in positions of power and influence.

We strongly concur with U. Thant's statement In response to the U.S. invasion of Cambodia 'I fear that if the parties involved do not take urgent, decisive and courageous measures towards peace, it will become increasingly difficult to end a war which constitutes a threat not only for the peoples of Indochina but for the whole of mankind.'

A.R. Bergen	W.D. Maurer	P. Smith
C.K. Birdsall	K.K. Mei	A.J. Thomasian
S.Chang	U.G. Montanari	G.L. Turin
L.A. Demetrius	W.G. Oldham	P.P. Varaiya
T.E. Duncan	J.K. Pollard	W.J. Walsh
R.W. Dutton	C.V. Ravi	W.J. Welch
A.C. English	G.Y. Robinson	J.R. Whinnery
A.Gill	R.A. Rohrer	R.M. White
T.K. Gustafson	P.M. Russo	J.C. Wiesner
C.W. Hartman	B.H. Sacks	E. Wong
A.M. Hopkin	S.E. Schwarz	L.A. Zadeh
A.J Lichtenberg	R.A. Skoog	A.R. Neureuther
M.A. Lieberman	O.J.M. Smith	

101

ROBERT E. WILLIAMS

(My home address)
May 27, 1970

Dear Sir:

Your note of May 8 concerning the action of the Electrical Engineering faculty and students is most disturbing. It would be well to consider why we are in Indochina. At the time of Korea, the forces of communism in the forty or so years preceding, had captured a third of the world's peoples and was threatening as they put it 'the masses of Asia'. Up until this time, we had done little to stop them.

In Korea, our government said "no more" and took a position between the aggressor and his victim - - not to capture for ourselves any territory but to make sure the aggressor didn't succeed.

We did the same thing in Vietnam. If we had wanted their territory, we'd have had it all by now. All our actions have been defensive in character.

Communism uses all kinds of weapons in its determination to conquer the world. What they can't win militarily, they will win psychologically. They intend to win.

The effectiveness of this part of the war, being fought in the U. S., can be analyzed by examining the results. They have 'captured' many Congressmen, Senators, students, educators, and much of our news media. If they can remove the last bastion of resistance, their vow that 'by 1973 the U. S. will fall into our hands like a ripe plum' will be a reality.

I used to think they would never pull it off. Now 1973 looks like a real possibility.

I realize and believe that your students are not 'radicals'. Certainly the learned minds on your faculty are not 'radicals'. You are 'deeply troubled', being 'sucked in', 'duped' by propaganda originating outside this country as a part of a campaign for world domination. These are harsh words, but think about it.

The 'agitators' behind your action, those with photos of Mao Tse-tung and Che Guevara in their rooms would have you believe our actions in Indochina are immoral and illegal. Consider the fact that you never hear about the aggressor, or his atrocities, the purges, the complete lack of free speech; or other immoral acts that go on in a communist country. They cry for 'peace', and appeal to the idealism of youth but their definition of peace is much different than the one you, the faculty, or the idealistic students would have. This is cruel deception.

If you allow them, nay, help them to succeed you may as your governor once said, 'one day, sit on the back porch with your grandson on your knee and tell him what it once was like in America when men were free.' That is if you survive the purge.

You would do well, if you are really troubled and concerned about America's future, to talk this over with your colleagues and do what you can to cut through the passion and bring reason back to your campus.

If my position is wrong, what do you lose? Very little if any thing. If your action is wrong; we may well lose our form of government which despite its faults has given man the most freedom he has ever enjoyed in all of his history.

What a shame that would be. I urge you to reconsider the eventual consequences of your action.

Sincerely,

Robert E. Williams

(Address)

Berkeley, California 94707
June 4, 1970
Mr. Robert E. Williams
(My home address)
Dear Mr. Williams:
Thank you for your letter of May 27, 1970. I appreciate the position you take as a member of our society who wishes responsible actions from educators. Copies of your letter are being made available to our students so they may better realize their problems in communicating their concerns to people in your position. Please remember that our students are living in a society which does not communicate well with them, even with those who are relatively moderate, and they are driven to strong statements in order to be heard. There is a need for listening on both sides, and for mutual understanding, if not agreement.

The students in our Department of Electrical Engineering and Computer Sciences also consider themselves a part of the responsible community that must keep operating in order to keep our society going. They are concerned, and they do seek to have someone listen to their voices with respect to these matters. They find themselves embedded in a society of young people, many of whom are more radical than they are, and they are working to divert the energies of this group toward constructive rather than destructive channels. Since our students started their efforts, there has been no violence on the Berkeley Campus in a time of violence elsewhere. I can only be proud of their activities.

Our students have not given up their efforts

toward obtaining a technical degree: they are making an extraordinary effort to communicate with the community at large at the same time as they seek to finish up their technical courses. In spite of some strongly worded rhetoric, most engineering students will leave the University in June with earned degrees or prepared to continue their education in the fall without delay or setback. Classes have not been closed in our Department, nor have courses been changed to political forums - which prevent students from getting technical education. The faculty has joined the students in this extraordinary activity, most of the faculty effort being directed to aiding the students in getting as much as possible from their technical courses. They have not 'copped out'.

The energy, materials, and postage required to send the original letter to you were not supplied directly or indirectly from University funds. The time was made available when the Governor of the State recessed the University for two days. The paper, cost of duplication, and postage were supplied by engineering students' donations.

I read things in press statements concerning what is happening at Berkeley which are not in accord with facts. I hope that if you read such things, you will not simply automatically accept everything you read about us in the papers.

Sincerely yours,

A. M. Hopkin
Professor and Acting Department
Chairman

Kent State University Student Mob Stage Riots - Four students, killed, 13 wounded

While the Berkeley radicals were considering their riot act and position on the national student riot, over in Ohio at Kent State University on Friday, May 1, 1970, the national student riot, called for by communists and answered by U.S. college students, was on. Students were demonstrating to protest the U.S. invasion of Cambodia. While the U.S. troops were being contained in Vietnam by our State Department, the VietCong were streaming out of Cambodia and killing American troops.

A copy of the U. S. Constitution was burned by the mob. On May 2, the mobsters swept through town throwing rocks and breaking windows, overwhelming the police. That evening over 1,000 students surrounded the ROTC barracks on the campus and burned it down. The mayor declared a state of emergency and called the governor who dispatched the National Guard, which by midnight had cleared the campus of demonstrators.

The next evening, Sunday, May 3, the demonstrators reassembled downtown, blocking traffic and refusing to disperse. The crowd became hostile. Tear gas was used and a number of people, Guardsmen and demonstrators, were injured.

Classes resumed on Monday, but the demonstrators were determined to hold a rally at noon, even if prohibited. An estimated two thousand people assembled on the Commons. Chants, curses and rocks answered an order to disperse. When tear gas failed, the Guard moved forward forcing the demonstrators up the hill onto an athletic practice field. Tear gas was traded for more rocks and verbal abuse.

The guardsmen were trapped by a fence on three sides and began a strategic retreat retracing their line of march. The screaming mob followed as close as 20 yards, accompanied by rocks and curses. At the top of the hill, a shot was heard, the guardsmen turned and fired between 61 an 67 rounds in 13 seconds. Only three Guardsman's rifles, set on automatic, in the hands of scared young soldiers being rushed by an angry mob of 2,000 Americans their own ages, would have been the recipe for disaster. Four persons lay dying and nine wounded. All were Kent State students. Some parents said, "They should have killed you all." A University ambulance moved through the campus making an announcement over the public address system. "By order of President White, the University is closed. Students should pack their things and leave the campus as soon as possible."

Later that day an injunction was obtained closing the University indefinitely. Normal campus activities did not resume until the summer session.

ROBERT E. WILLIAMS

Rioters Back on Stage May 2003

"The Revolutionary Worker" issue #1199 of May 18, 2003, (apparently a communist webpage) reported that over 300 students gathered at Kent State for a remembrance march on the 33rd anniversary of May 4, 1970, when rioters lost their lives. Kent State officials disapproved of the march on the grounds it might cause a disturbance or violence.

The students marched anyway attracting students from Ohio, Pennsylvania and Michigan, and they listened to speeches about how the U.S. continues to carry out wars against people like the bombing and occupation of Iraq. The professors and other intellectuals spoke out against the roundups of Muslims, Arabs and South Asian people and the repression here in America since 9/11.

It is the same as the 60s — Americans lining up on the side of the enemy. What else is new?

APPENDIX B

Brainwashing

Prisoners of War in Korea — a practical exercise in living under Communism

The following is the exact copy of a speech presented by Dr. William E. Mayer, psychiatrist with the rank of major in the U.S. Army on November 27, 1956, at a Conference of Professors of Air Science at Maxwell Air Force Base. Major Mayer has extensive experience in psychiatry and was assigned to the Special Intelligence Project on Korean prisoners of War and interviewed most of the prisoners of war we got back out of Korea.

His speech gives us a good view of the Communist control system and explains how the Communists were able to control over 7,000 American prisoners that in previous wars were the most recalcitrant prisoners imaginable, as well as exercise control over a third of the world without major problems.

It also gives some insight into the approach used in persuading Americans to support Communist causes. Radical students and even university professors would reportedly take groups of students down to the local beer garden to drink beer they had provided and lead them in guided discussions, "self criticism," if you will, against America, the Korean and Vietnam Wars, our leaders, and in support or tolerance of, or joining, those who would bring America down.

Simple psychology, but very effective.

My fellow schoolteachers –

I am conscious of a very great privilege, and I say that in all earnestness, for the simple reason that I think you people have the most important job in the Air Force and as you know I am not here recruiting or any such thing.

However, we have become concerned in the Army, as I think many of you have in your branch, about certain trends and tendencies among personnel reflecting on the qualities of leadership and moral fiber.

We have done a lot of study on it as have your own people. We have hired a great many intelligence civilian research groups to do more study. As a nation we are about as confused about personnel management and leadership and moral fiber and right and wrong as parents are confused about whether or not to spank their children.

I am going to talk about our findings with the Americans, who were the first large cross-section of American youth to live in a Communist society for any period of time.

There were altogether 7,000 such people of whom we finally got back 4,000. My comments will be restricted almost entirely to Army personnel — about 95% of the prisoners in Korea.

I want to share with you what happened to them in relation to a specific document namely the Code of Conduct. This remarkable and rather curious document has been in existence a little over a year. It was thought important enough by the President that he announced it himself instead of leaving it to the Chiefs of Staff. It is a greatly maligned and greatly under-estimated piece of work. It is probably the least understood military document that I have ever seen, judging by people's reaction to it, even intelligent and sophisticated people.

What I will actually present to you in a very abbreviated form this afternoon is a coverage of the data that went into the construction of the Code of Conduct in the first place. And I am hoping very sincerely that in hearing this version of what we know, and what we think we know, we can make application relative to this document in the critically important area of the junior officer with whom you deal and who you really prepare from the standpoint of attitude.

I have a document which I would like to read for you, by way of introduction. It is fairly brief. It is very much to the point. It was written by Communists, but I would like for you to listen to it in as detached and objective a way as possible.

Most of it came from a message that was written by the Chief of Intelligence of the Chinese Peoples' Volunteers in Korea to the Chief of Intelligence of the Chinese Peoples' Republic in Peking. The original one that we got was entitled *An Evaluation of American Soldiers.*

The text literally translated is as follows:

"Based upon our observation of the American soldiers and their officers captured in this war for the liberation of Korea from Capitalist Imperialist aggression some facts are evident:

- The American soldier has weak loyalties to his family, his religion, his country and to his fellow soldiers.
- His concept of right and wrong is hazy.
- He is basically materialistic and he is an opportunist. By himself he feels insecure and frightened.
- He under-estimates his own worth and his strength and his ability to survive.
- He is ignorant of social values, social concepts and tensions. There is little or no knowledge or understanding, even among American university graduates of U.S. political history and philosophy, federal, state and community organizations, civil rights, freedoms and safeguards and how these allegedly operate within his own decadent system. He is exceedingly insular and provincial with little or no idea of the problems and aims of what he contemptuously describes as foreigners and their countries.
- He has an unrealistic concept of American eternal and inherent, rather than earned or proven, superiority and absolute military invincibility.
- He fails to appreciate the meaning of, and the necessity for, military organization or any form of discipline. Most often he appears to feel that his military service is a hateful unavoidable servitude to be tolerated as briefly as possible and escaped from as rapidly as possible, or he is what they themselves call a peacetime soldier. He sees it only as a soft and a safe job.

- He resents hardship and sacrifice of any description as if these things were unreasonable and unfair to him personally.
- Based upon the above facts about the Imperialist United States aggressors the re-education and indoctrination program for American prisoners proceeds as planned."

And that's the end of the message.

That is obviously a Communist document. I do not present it as an endorsement of the document. I only present it for your consideration and because it contributes a good bit to the understanding of the approach the Communists used in their handling of the Americans in Korea.

There has been a great deal of tripe produced in this country and abroad about the nature of Communist captivity and the nature of suffering in the Communist world.

I am not here to deny that suffering exists in the Communist system. I am here to offer an observation, and it is only an opinion, that we will never really be able to combat with great success what the Communists attempt to do, until we understand them on something more than an epithetical, name-calling kind of a basis.

In Korea was our first magnificent attempt really to understand them and to understand something about life in a Communist society, not from the standpoint of horror stories and star chambers, but from the standpoint of what goes on with the average individual, if there is such a thing, who lives in a Communist state.

So we set to work to evaluate the Americans who came back. Unfortunately most of the information given to the public and to the military has for a variety of usually sincere, not always wise, reasons been presented from the standpoint of the old name-calling approach.

The stories that have made the best printing and the best reading and sell the most editions of *True* magazine emphasize the horrors, the degradations and the brutality of the Communists. All of this is true but none of which gives the typical or insightful picture of Communist life.

The Communists had in their hands over 7,000 American soldiers, behind their own lines on a peninsula, where it was just as hard to chase somebody as it was to run away.

They had first and foremost the same objective with these people as they have in any Communist society on earth — namely the physical control of the people.

It became clear as we did our study that this overwhelmingly was their principal objective — they had secondary objectives of great importance particularly, most dramatically, the exploitation of Air Force representatives on the basis of charges of germ warfare.

However this still was secondary to the great need to handle these 7,000 recalcitrant Americans who in previous wars had, and rightfully so, the general reputation of being the most difficult prisoners to keep in any camp anyplace.

So they set about to do it and they used a procedure which we find described by number of experts, real and self appointed, under the general term of "brainwashing."

Brainwashing is a word that the government dislikes, frankly, and in a way I go along with it because it can mean anything to anybody from what you say to a girl out on a date to something the Communists attempt to do with their people.

However the word deserves a little attention. It is a magnificent psychological achievement in itself as it creates an aura of irresistibility, of magic, of something that happens to people's minds.

Indeed brainwashing, as it is generally accepted by those who seem to know the most about it, including one Edward Hunter who originally introduced the word into the language, does include a fair proportion of strange things like the handling of Cardinal Minzenty and Otis and Vogeler and some of Colonel Arnold's experiences and so on.

However brainwashing includes a great deal more, but for the most part for the great bulk of the prisoners, brainwashing was a process of indoctrination and a very excellent one. It employed in a careful, systematic and thoughtful way the same principles of psychology and psychiatry that we use not only in treating patients but in education.

They used these in a more determined sense than we have attempted to apply our psychological principles socially. Social psychiatry is a new thing in this country. It is beginning to crop up in departments in medical schools.

We are beginning to realize that there is a lot more to this business of human beings and their feelings than just what comes out on the couch. There is something that goes on between people and among people in groups.

The Communists haven't discovered ultimate truth in this business, but they have devoted a great deal of attention to the application of psychological principles in a way we consider backward, in a way designed not to restore people to emotional equilibrium or to help them to a better, more mature adjustment — but basically to interfere with what we consider normal adult, happy relationships between people and this more than anything else is brainwashing.

Essentially it is a weapon because it is the most effective to date control system, dictatorship-wise, that we have ever seen in operation. It is a peculiar kind of weapon of course in that it is being used right today. It is being used in differing degrees here in this country as well as abroad. It can be used on your friends as well as your enemies.

It is particularly good for neutrals and determined neutralists like people in India and Indonesia. Its effectiveness I think can be judged pragmatically by a glance at the results of Communist methods.

In the now thirty nine years since the October Revolution the Communists have taken over from scratch, and now control, one-out-of-every-three living human beings. They control these people with more success, less apparent trouble than anybody has ever controlled any really large numbers of people.

Now they have trouble, no question about it. They have trouble, beautiful trouble in Hungary and in Poland and in East Germany, but the remarkable thing is they have so little in the forty years that they have taken over and now control these 900 million people.

Now they have done this by the use of a good deal of fairly liberal bloodshed. I heard from a non-classified but intelligent source not long ago that we can with absolute authority say that the Chinese alone have killed over 20 million out of the total they have in that country. Which isn't perhaps a large percentage but is an awful lot of people.

The fact remains, however, that any evaluation of the number of people so treated in the Communist societies all over the earth still leaves large groups of humans who have never been handled in this fashion, have never been exiled to Siberia, beaten or tortured or even separated from their families, who show a remarkable degree of acquiescence to what the Communists are doing.

We think this weapon has a great deal to do with it — this application of perfectly sound psychological principles.

We found, first of all — and this has been a point of great controversy for a variety of reasons — that the weapon as it was first employed on Americans did not for the great majority include any of the standard techniques which we expected and which we consciously and deliberately attempted to elicit for use in protest at an international political level.

Thinking back the average soldier in a bunker on the front lines in Korea pretty well expected that if he were caught by this diabolical oriental enemy he would surely have fingernails abused during his initial de-briefings, he would probably be subjected to all kinds of exquisite oriental abuses. Partly because of the legend that exists in our country about the oriental and partly it was based on the realistic considerations of how Japanese treated many Americans during WWII.

However the Americans found, for the great majority, there was no such thing. There was no physical abuse we can identify as ever being deliberate or systematic for about 99% of the total group of prisoners.

There was no narcotics used on these people. You know the Chinese have a great deal to do with the international narcotics traffic. They didn't use magic, and by magic I include Pavlov's conditioned reflex, a process invented by a Russian for physiological experimentation, which is a very interesting one and which gives us some insight about learning in general.

Certainly the conditioned reflex plays a part in certain aspects of human learning but does not account for acceptance of that concept on the part of a complicated human being operating in an even more complicated social environment.

The reason I labor the point is because a number of, I think, competent psychologists in this country as well as abroad have said that the Communists' great strength with people and their ability to communicate their ideas rests with the fact that they have perverted and magnified the Pavlovian conditioned reflex to where you can no more resist their political machinations than Pavlov's dogs can resist salivating — which is just plain hogwash.

Finally they didn't use beautiful young females to lead these innocent young soldiers astray. The sex approach which was attempted in some American universities by the Young Communist League in the 30s has apparently gone by the board along with legalized abortion and several other experiments in the Peoples' Democracies.

What they did do with the majority of Americans, and remember I am restricting this discussion to the experiences of Army personnel, leaving out, at least for the time, the Air Force people who were held in solitary some of whom in Manchuria were subjected to every known form of crude physical and mental abuse to try to get them to cooperate.

I am talking instead about the rest of the prisoners. For them the procedure of brainwashing was a remarkably simple and deceptive kind of a thing.

The procedure that was actually used on these people began for most of them about the time they were captured. It began first of all with a speech of welcome and introduction.

The speech was given at collecting points usually with groups of ten or fifteen or twenty American soldiers. After being often inadequately disarmed, they were gathered together and then a young Chinese appeared, normally not in military dress. A Chinese who was young, who affected a friendly and conciliatory attitude and gave the following little speech and I repeat it almost verbatim:

He would say approximately:

"We welcome you to the ranks of the people. We are happy and privileged to have liberated you from the Imperialist Wall Street war mongers who started this war.

We have nothing against you personally. We know you don't want to be here any more than we do. We are not going to abuse you. We are going instead to offer you a proposition — a deal — a fair shake.

The deal is this — you cooperate with us physically. Don't get any ideas about our being your enemy. After all we are really the people like you are. Listen to us — let us present to you our side of the world picture today — of what we think is really going on here in Korea and back in your homes and with the great masses of people you have never had a chance to learn about.

And that's what we ask of you. In return for this there will be no slave camps, no work gangs, no road crews, no coal mines — we will just simply give you a chance to learn the truth as we know the truth to be.

We are not even going to insist that you accept it. We ask only that you hear us out, which is only American fair play, and make up your own minds about what is true, and then as soon as the war mongers allows this senseless slaughter of innocent civilians to be ended we want you to go home to your own good homes and fine families and tell them the truth as you understand the truth to be."

That's fair enough and it is a whole lot better than having your fingernails pulled out.

Right after this they set about to isolate and segregate certain groups. They separated, first of all, all colored troops — put them in separate camps. The U. S. Army had officially ended segregation — all the branches of service — but these were Army people.

The second group they segregated was what they called the poisonous individualists — anybody who showed any kind of leadership tendencies.

Anybody who had the audacity to assume that he could lead other men within this specially constructed social organization was immediately dubbed a poisonous individualist or hopeless reactionary and put off in what they called a Reactionary Camp — a camp more heavily guarded, in general less well fed, less intensely schooled but still not particularly abusive by POW standards.

Our first and most disturbing finding in general about the prisoners of war was that it was only necessary to segregate one in every twenty American fighting men — this includes officers, NCOs and enlisted men — to deprive the other 95% of any effective leadership.

Only one in twenty thought it worthwhile to try to act on the basis of organization, of taking command or responding to command.

They then had a group of 95% of the American soldiers leaderless. With this group they set about their applied group psychology, and not very mysterious psychology at that, designed basically to do one thing and one thing only. Please remember that the major objective of the Communist society is the physical control of the society whether it is a group of POWs or cell of a Communist Party in Montgomery or New York City or in Peking.

For the purpose of physical control the best possible military principle is the same one that is ancient and hallowed and that is "divide and conquer" and so they set out to divide these people in a most peculiar kind of a way.

Their objective very much resembles the kind of thing that a patient says to the psychiatrist when he walks in under his own steam for treatment. And I am not talking about very sick people. I am talking about the great majority of psychiatric patients who are still able to function, who are still responsible citizens, but who are also upset and who feel finally that they need help.

They come in and their complaints frequently, if not always, will revolve around certain areas of human life. Their most common expression is "Doctor, people don't understand me." and certainly you and I have felt this way. Secondly they often report they no longer communicate successfully or rewardingly with people who have been important to them.

"My wife and I don't have anything to talk about anymore. We don't seem to understand each other."

"I don't like the people I work with in the office but I can't put my finger on why."

"I am not happy in my job but I don't know what I'd rather do."

This is a very typical constellation for the psychiatric patient who walks into your office to present for you in some form or other.

This was exactly what we saw among returning prisoners of war. When we got a large number of them, about five hundred, in Tokyo, we put them on an open ward the ambulatory ward in the Tokyo hospital.

A few of them were quite sick but a great number of them could walk around and were not restricted from a medical point of view.

Those of you who have ever walked down a ward in a military hospital holding ambulatory patients know that the ward has certain characteristics. One, it is noisy. Two, the noise is being produced by a small number of people because that's all the people that are ever on the ward. They are usually at the Red Cross or chasing around downtown or anything their ambulatory status will permit.

The peculiar thing about these people was if you walked on a ward at the Tokyo Army Hospital with maybe fifty POWs, all fifty would be on the ward, which is just unheard of.

The second thing that was noticeable was the wards were quiet. They weren't chasing the nurse or the Red Cross worker, they weren't making jokes, they weren't playing cards, radios were not on very loud.

And the third thing that was noticeable was they were all by themselves as much as you could possibly be on a large open ward. They weren't gathered together in groups. When they were given passes to go downtown, they went downtown by themselves. And you know soldiers never go downtown by themselves. But these guys did — the less than one-out-of five who accepted the pass to go downtown.

And the next thing we noted was, though they wouldn't talk to one another, they would talk to us, almost compulsively, You couldn't stop them once they started. They would talk, and talk, and talk and say things that we just never expected to hear people say about each another. Not vicious nasty things — they just simply seemed unable to determine what might be harmful to say about somebody else, and they would talk and talk but not to each other. To the doctor, the nurse, the intelligence agent, the corpsman —- to anybody, except another prisoner of war.

This we had never before seen. We know that prisoners of war develop intense emotional alliances with one another; they survive frequently on the basis of what we call the buddy system; the alliances often last for many, many years after they are repatriated. They do have some peculiar reactions when first freed — anybody would — but they got over these fairly rapidly — usually.

Not these people. In the last year I have talked to over 200 ex-prisoners of war. The one consistent thing about them was some of these attitudes persist, particularly the sense of isolation from other people.

This can be done in a calculated, deliberate sort of a way and this is how:

It is only necessary to interfere with, and corrupt seriously, the process of human communication in order to accomplish this. They set about it in standard classical ways which are being used today in the Communist Party USA, which are used even in the Kremlin and which involves chiefly INFORMING and a process called SELF CRITICISM.

We have heard about kids in a Communist society informing on their parents and I am sure you have dismissed this as the kind of accusation we make against people that are pretty inhuman. This accusation, within certain limits, is an entirely true and entirely feasible kind of a thing for the simple reason that informing in the Communist state is not informing in the democratic society. They are entirely different procedures.

In the People's democracy informing is undertaken as a civic and social responsibility — as an exercise of your responsibility not to the people in charge but the people, period — to your fellows, to your class of which you are nothing but a fragment.

Informing was undertaken, not viciously, but for the welfare of the group in the POW camp. Informing done on somebody who stole a turnip and should have shared it, or took somebody's blanket when it should have been shared, or who didn't use the latrine properly. This kind of informing was quickly and tangibly rewarded. Remember the Communist evaluation that we are opportunistic — we will do things for reward — particularly material ones.

So they rewarded the informer materially but they also rewarded them with status and approval. And then — and this is really the crux of the success of the system — they failed apparently to punish the man who was informed upon. At least in the beginning.

Now they didn't let him escape "scot-free." He was taken aside by one of the Chinese instructors, the same guys who had made the initial welcoming address, a man who spoke not pidgin English but Columbia University English, or Chicago, or California English.

A man who had been here and seen our Cadillacs and big buildings and who was still a Communist, and who was called an instructor, would take the culprit aside and have a little heart-to-heart chat with him — which struck most prisoners as being kind of a kindergarten type of procedure. He was made to see the error of his ways, confess that he had done wrong, recant and assert his determination not to repeat this ant-social behavior in the future. Having done this he was off the hook — at least in the early part of the war.

Sometimes he was asked to write his confession or self criticism, Everybody thought this was a harmless kind of a thing. It didn't hurt anybody to get informed upon so nobody got mad enough to beat up or drown the informer as has been routine in other American prisoner of war camps.

The result was that by the end of the first year of the war, as far as we can determine, there was one reliable American informer in every group of about ten American prisoners — one that we can now name. That's just an awful lot of informers!

Some of the prisoners reported that there was one in every squad and squads were frequently four or five men. The result was what they were after. The result was simply that the soldier discovered that he couldn't be sure about anybody. You can always be sure about the man who hates you. You know where you stand. But when a perfectly nice guy, out of a sense of civic responsibility or a desire for two tailor-made cigarettes informs upon you, even though you don't get hurt, it begins to seriously disrupt your interpersonal relationships and you back off from other people.

And of course that was exactly what happened. Men began to back off into one of the most perfect solitary confinement cells ever conceived - not of steel and concrete but an emotional solitary confinement cell.

The process of Self Criticism is a part of this same Informing kind of a cultural organization only it is more collectivized and formalized. It is a seminar type group of ten or twelve people. This is done in the Kremlin — actually. it is done in every unit of the platoon size of the Chinese Army as was related to us by the prisoners we got on the front lines.

Self-criticism is simply a corruption of religious confession — in another sense a corruption of group psychiatric treatment. Each man is required to get up in this small and seemingly harmless group of other Americans and discuss his shortcomings, his failures and particularly his poor attitudes.

Every officer in the military service knows that while you can handle all kinds of misbehavior, when it comes to attitude, there is a limit.

But the Chinese handled them in this peculiar and carefully thought-out way. You confess your own bad attitudes. Having confessed them, again, there is a sense of having expiated your guilt. A sense also of having been accepted by the rest of the group. It is a getting-it-off-your-chest sort of thing that couldn't have been more harmless. And of course it was perfectly harmless, for the first week. Because everybody thought these confessions which the Chinese so childishly demanded were very superficial and kind of humorous and everybody listened and kind of smiled and took his turn and got up and talked.

And then all of a sudden something very peculiar happened, something inevitable happened. And that is, that the men began to notice that the other men were listening, and they also began to notice a feeling in themselves of having talked too much. When asked, the soldier would say "I don't know what I talked too much about, but I did have the feeling I had gone too far. I had exposed more of myself than I had intended." This was exactly, of course, what the men had done. Ultimately you run out of superficial things and you talk about things that may not on the surface be serious, but are meaningful to you, and once you begin to do this, you become vulnerable and exposed, and you back off from other people.

We see this in group psychotherapy, in group treatment, unless it is carefully managed and carefully controlled.

We seen this in our own society, more often generally speaking among women than among men. But in our society women handle it better than men. They do exactly what the soldier does when he felt he had gone too far and exposed too much of their own personal business. They simply set about immediately to collect an equivalent amount of intelligence about their listener and that is the origin of the armed truce.(laughs).

And this is exactly what these nineteen- and twenty-year old American GIs were doing with each other. They came back with fabulous amounts of information about other prisoners, but they wouldn't talk to them walking around the compound and they wouldn't get together with them because you see, you really couldn't be sure of these people.

One final thing they did to isolate men from one another and from the usual sources of emotional support was the control of their mail in what must have been one of the most difficult, boring job of censorship that was ever undertaken by anybody.

As you perhaps know we delivered large amounts of mail to Panmunjom for further delivery to the prisoners. The Chinese evidently read each and every piece of mail that was ever given to them for further delivery.

We had written both in psychiatric and non-professional literature a good bit about the value of mail to the soldier overseas. Certainly each of us know what mail can do to men. We see the infantryman sometimes upon the receipt of a "Dear John letter" become either useless or practically suicidal in his carelessness. We see all kinds of reactions about mail.

The Chinese know just how important it is as well as we do, so they undertook their censorship in a new and peculiar kind of a way. Rather than cutting anything out of letters — which is very irritating as I sure you can recall — or black out certain sentences or words, they simply withheld any letter that was from an emotional and psychological standpoint, the kind the prisoners really desperately needed.

Consider for a moment he is getting no emotional support from his daily interpersonal relationships. He is not getting the re-assurance that you and I get from our relationships with friends. He isn't certain of himself, of his worth, and of course this is a typical reaction, anyway, of being confined. The person who is confined usually has serious self-doubts. After awhile he wonders why he survived and his fellows didn't survive — what right he has, so to speak, to represent the others. Volumes have been written about this one phenomenon of captivity.

And there is nothing better for this than to get a letter from home, particularly the old-fashioned trite kind of letter that says, "We love you, and we are waiting for you, and don't worry about anything at home. Everything is all right, and we pray for you every night. Just take care of yourself." The kind of mail no prisoner ever received as far as we could determine.

123

Nor did he ever get to see a snapshot if one was sent, but a Dear John letter, if it were sent, he got. Or a divorce notice, if it managed to get mailed, he got. Prisoners got notices from collection companies on the Yalu River sometimes within four weeks of the time it was posted in the United States.

They particularly liked, and we have one really superb example of this, they particularly liked a letter from a wife which could be really emotionally disturbing. The one case that comes to mind was an army major who had married rather late in life in his mid-forties to a 20-year old German girl during the occupation of Germany. She was a really ravishing girl — she was a beautiful person. He had never felt certain of himself in his relationship with women to begin with. He was very devoted to this youngster, he brought her back to the States, of course, but he was never sure she came back because she loved him, or whether she married him to get back to the States. He was somewhat insecure we would say in psychiatry.

He left her to go to Korea — left her with his family in New York. She wrote him daily, devotedly; he never got a letter. She never got any of his. After about a year and a half of "not knowing," the girl in desperation wrote one letter complaining, letting her hair down, and announcing incidentally that she had met an awfully nice young man who said he was an artist in Hollywood, and wanted her to come there to model, and so she was leaving New York.

This soldier told us that up until that point he behaved like a man but from that point on there just really wasn't any point in it.

Now that is not an over-simplified or contrived example — this is a true case of an American soldier. This is what in a sense, the Communists on a somewhat limited scale, were trying to achieve with everybody. And they did.

When we had the soldiers back in Tokyo and the Red Cross came by with all their money, they offered the people the opportunity to call the United States, not at five dollars a minute or four (whatever it was from Tokyo then) but free. Call anybody you like, for free. This is part of our approach to their having been a prisoner of war — it was sort of an automatic assumption that having been a prisoner you were a hero. This was psychologically destructive to the POW, I might add.

At any rate, they were given this particular benefit and more than half of the prisoners offered this opportunity flatly refused. You didn't have to call your family or wife. Call anybody at Red Cross expense. More that half said no. Maybe tomorrow, maybe next week, maybe somebody else would rather use the phone. But they wouldn't call home.

Well, this essentially is brainwashing. This is an attempt to strip individuals of their normal sources of emotional support which is gotten in a simple, elemental kind of way. We get it from our association with others, from what we invest in other people, and what they invest in us.

This creates a kind of a vacuum when you are isolated as these people were and herein lies one explanation for the almost religious devotion to this ideology which is manifest on the part of a great many Communists. Into this vacuum must be introduced something, and in these camps they introduced an education. A rather condensed intensive sort of education very much like, in many ways, that which is given in Communist societies all over the world.

An education that supplants to some extent the relationship with human beings, an education that gives you something to invest in emotionally, to believe in, to draw support from. And the fact that you get your support from it makes it mandatory that when the line changes out of the Kremlin you change with it, with a minimum of resistance, as we have commonly seen for the last ten years.

The education that was given these people I can't possibly begin to describe in this brief period. It was methodologically an excellent one usually every graduate teaching method we have ever observed.

I would like to remind you that the overall educational level in the United States among men coming into the army is the first semester of the ninth grade. These people have not been exposed to much in the way of formal education.

They were given an education, however, which used for its method the seminar, the guest speaker, the group discussion, the dramatization of principles, the interpretative production of dramatics. *Uncle Tom's Cabin* was used as the first production in most camps. Not only did they play up the racial controversy, but they painted Simon Legree as the prototype of all capitalists.

They weren't disheartened by the absence of understanding of the average American about his own system. They assumed he didn't know much about it, so they set out to teach him about how it supposedly worked. They compared it often with the kinds of things they were trying to teach in the Peoples' Democracy, and they taught him the true version of history, the truth being understood only by the ideological advanced members of the Communist Party.

This truthful version of history contained a great many truthful things, about us as well as other Capitalist Imperialist countries. They taught for example about the Opium Wars that Great Britain fought — oh they were only small wars but they did fight them with some Chinese who had officially refused to buy any more opium. This was, of course, a very long time ago; it was about a hundred years ago.

They talked about more recent abuses within the capitalist economic society. They talked for example about the Oklahoma farmers who immigrated to the Imperial Valley and worked for a dollar a day — that is the whole family worked for a dollar a day. Now that wasn't very long ago. They talked about the sweat shops where clothing is made in New York. They talked about the minimum wage law which does not apply in certain states in the United States. They held up, magnified, distorted, but always started with something that was demonstrable, something they thought hey could make political hay with.

They taught about the UN, they taught about how our Southern Fleet and our entry into Korea violated the UN Charter. They taught about Harry Truman and the capitalists supporting him.

They had art classes for those who wanted to draw pictures rather than just go to school all the time, because if you could draw the kind of pictures they liked, they paid you for it. They reprinted your pictures; we found some of them in *Crocodile*. We got pictures drawn by Americans in Communist publications in the United States, pictures like Harry Truman with bloody dripping claws gathering up us exploited tools of the Wall Street warmongers and throwing us into the jaws of death in Korea.

They encouraged newspaper articles for camp newspapers, particularly if you could write really good articles like the one:

"I wish to extend my profound gratitude to the Peoples' Volunteer Army for teaching me to read and write English, because in the Capitalist Imperialist Society of Pittsburgh from which I come, only the sons of rich capitalists are allowed to read and write English."

— signed Private John Smith, U. S. Army

We saw this and we got concerned about John Smith, and we waited for him to come home. We asked him about his article, and he admitted freely that he had written it. He said, "It couldn't do any harm since it was not true. In a way, it could almost be considered true, but anyway the people in Pittsburgh knew it wasn't true, so it couldn't really hurt anybody."

But of course, what John didn't realize is that the 900 million people who get nothing but this approach don't know it is a lie. And the second 900 million people, the second third of the world who haven't quite decided which side they will be on, they don't know it's a lie, either.

It wasn't just John — it was a hundred Johns or several hundred of these people — who wrote these articles in a more or less innocent way, because after all, they were paying for such articles.

This was the education. It was something that occupied the attention and the emotional energy of these men, who are not today Communists or even security risks. It was simply of interest to us for the following reasons:

First we saw the results. The results were briefly this. No Americans in these community camps, subjected to nothing more than this kind of control, in camps as lightly guarded as one armed guard to a hundred soldiers, with no machine gun towers, no search lights, no complicated electrical barbed wire fences, no vicious Doberman Pinchers — out of those men in those camps of more than four thousand people, not one American ever escaped from an organized prison camp in Korea. Ever. In spite of what you hear on TV.

127

That was a disturbing finding. Our second disturbing finding about the results of this program was there was never any effective, sustained, organized resistance of any kind. There were sporadic outbursts of resistance. There was heroic behavior by a great many Americans individually, but as a military procedure, almost, or for practical purposes, never.

And then we found the people died under this system. You didn't have to put the branding iron on them, and you didn't have to starve them systematically. They were underfed, they were given no medical attention to speak of except the implantation of a piece of contaminated chicken liver under the skin of the chest, in case you had any disease whatever. But you had to volunteer for that.

They were given inadequate shelter and poor clothing, but still the conditions of captivity were, as far as we can determine, infinitely better than those in Japanese POW camps in WWII and were better than most of the German POW camps.

And yet men died, and they died in large numbers. They died in a ratio of four-out-of-every-ten American prisoners captured, died in captivity — 38% to be absolutely accurate. That is a highest death rate of Americans in any prison camp or any prison in any war, in any time of our history since the American Revolution.

This constitutes a real, genuine problem. Plus the fact that instead of occupying hundreds of guards, only a few were occupied. The others were down on the 38th Parallel shooting at other American soldiers — which is a pretty good way to wage a war you will have to admit.

Because of all this the Code was written. This Code of Conduct that everybody says is only 247 English words and isn't going to change anybody's behavior, and certainly you people, who work with youngsters and troops know that by the time we get them their attitudes are pretty well formed, know this is true. We are sure not going to spout high sounding principles at people and expect to make perfect military machines. That isn't at all what the Code of Conduct was created for, what it has in mind, or what it will accomplish.

The Code simply points out point-by-point where in this kind of personnel management system we are vulnerable. Neither the Code nor I attempt to imply there is some basic defect in Americans. Nor does the Code tend to reaffirm what the Communists accuse us of in the original document that I read you.

However, we know that more than a third of the Americans by their own admission under this system and no other duress, either confessed to things that weren't true, communicated or actively collaborated with the enemy, took part in peace campaigns, wrote home to their mothers and their newspapers begging them to join movements for peace to stop this senseless slaughter of innocent civilians by the U.S. Air Force, I might add, which is what they always say.

Soldiers took part in this, under no more duress than this. They did things that by historical standards of military behavior were, if not illegal at least tragic.

The Code points these out one by one.

It says for example:

I will continue to resist if I am captured. Why? Well, for psychological reasons in the face of intense fear or anxiety all you can do is either run or fight. And if you can't run that moment, you have got to fight if you will remain integrated emotionally. You have got to resist, even symbolically. And further, resistance against that you consider evil, and this is a terrible word for a psychologist to use, is a moral principle. It has something to do with the perseverance that is taught to a child. It has to do with a system of values and believing in something.

Heroism is no longer an MGM type production. There is no such thing. The only kind of effective resistance is a function of the faith and loyalty among individuals and it has to be undertaken by groups.

And so it is also with the Escape proposition we are teaching now. Do you know why people never escaped in Korea? No escape committees! It's perfectly simple. You can't escape by yourself. There were some heroic attempts. The closest to success that anybody got was an young Air Force lieutenant in connection with an old beat up civilian newspaper man. He almost got out and it was a tribute to the tremendous devotion to one another that they almost did. Only disease prevented that success.

The soldier would be thinking about escaping and somebody would come up to him and say. "We know you are thinking about escaping, and we don't think you ought to do this because they will take it out on the rest of us."

Which may be true. When you drive your tank up to where they are shooting, they will try to take it out on everybody in that tank, if they can hit you.

And so people didn't escape — no escape committees.

Another principle in the Code says, *"If I am ever captured by an enemy, I will not accept favors from him"*

That's only perfectly logical, isn't it? Everything in the whole Code is. You cannot compromise with something you think is evil or wrong. This is not a military subject. This is taught in childhood. This is in the Code because some men thought they could make a deal.

A Lt. Colonel, graduate of a service academy, told me that he thought that by collaborating with the enemy, or giving that appearance, he could exercise a beneficial effect on behalf of the other prisoners. Now you can interpret that anyway you want — a rationalism, an excuse, an out-and-out lie — needless to say, regardless of his motivation, he just ended up collaborating and not helping the other prisoners at all.

When you think you can make a deal, you are heading for an awful lot of trouble.

Then there is a point in the Code about *keeping faith with other prisoners.* Does anybody have to tell any old soldier in this room that he has to keep faith with other Americans — not to do anything to hurt them?

Do you know why that point is in the Code? Remember the 38% of the prisoners who died. They died in most cases because if a man was too sick to eat, nobody bothered to feed him.

And there is the case of Sgt. Gallagher. He threw two sick men out of the hut because they were stinking up the hut. They had dysentery very badly. And of course, we know this exhortation in the Code is not going to change Sgt. Gallagher a bit. He was a bully. He threw those people out of the hut when it was 30 degrees below zero, and they died in about an hour. He was convicted of murder about a year ago here in New York.

The Code was not built for Sgt. Gallagher. It was built for those other forty men who stood there and watched him throw them out.

We asked the soldiers, "What were you doing when Gallagher threw those men out in the cold?"

"Well, sir, I was just bundled up there in the hut trying to keep warm like everybody else."

"Oh, you knew it was cold then?"

"Yes, sir."

"And didn't you think it would hurt those guys to be thrown out in the snow when they were sick?"

"Well, sure."

"So what did you do about it?" we asked.

"Well, nothing, sir."

"And why not, soldier?"

"Well, sir, because it wasn't any of my business."

And so Americans died, and Americans collaborated and Americans didn't escape because it wasn't any of other Americans' business.

So there is something in the Code about keeping faith with other Americans. This has nothing more to do with Communist captivity than it does with flying a plane from here to New York, where three or four people have to cooperate or it won't fly.

END of tape

U. S. Military Code of Conduct

The Code of Conduct for U. S. Armed Forces was first published by President Dwight D. Eisenhower in Executive Order 10631 in 1955. It was later amended by President Carter in 1977. It outlines the basic responsibilities and obligations of all U.S. service members in the United States.

I

I am an American, fighting in the forces which guard my country and our way of life. I am prepared to give my life in their defense.

II

I will never surrender of my own free will. If I am in command, I will never surrender the members of my command while they still have the means to resist.

III

If I am captured I will continue to resist by all means available. I will make every effort to escape and aid others to escape. I will accept neither parole nor special favors from the enemy.

IV

If I become a prisoner of war, I will keep faith with my fellow prisoners. I will give no information or take part in any action which might be harmful to my comrades. If I am senior I will take command. If not I will obey the lawful orders of those appointed over me and will back them up in every way.

V

When questioned, should I become a prisoner of war, I am required to give name, rank, service number, and date of birth. I will evade answering further questions to the utmost of my ability. I will make no oral or written statements

disloyal to my country and its allies or harmful to their cause.

VI

I will never forget that I am an American, fighting for freedom, responsible for my actions, and dedicated to the principles which made my country free. I will trust in my God and in the United States of America.

APPENDIX C

A Different View of Watergate

The *Dallas Morning News* editorial of Saturday, April 23, 1994, on the occasion of the death of Richard M. Nixon, talked of his triumphs, and particularly of his insecurities. The writer asked, "Why else were the President and his men driven to dirty tricks when a 1972 victory over George McGovern was as certain as day following night?"

Maybe this is why. It is no secret that President Nixon was an avid anti-communist. By 1950 communism had conquered a third of the world, and was working on the rest of it. He knew of the communist vow, "Your grandchildren will live under socialism, and you won't even know how it happened."

Nixon was to become very suspicious of, and to feel he was a target of, the media. He was a member of Congress in the late 1940s, and early 1950s, when a number of Hollywood actors, actresses, writers, directors, producers and news commentators came under fire from the House Un-American Activities Committee for their activities in support of Communist Front Organizations and/or of being communists themselves. Ronald Reagan, then head of the Screen Actors Guild was among the witnesses and later as President would call Russia the "evil empire."

Approximately 280 were fired and blackballed, and ten were convicted of acts so severe they were sent to jail for a year. All eventually returned to work. The media now calls it the blackest moment in American history. Many agree, but for a different reason. Were some innocent or duped? Probably. Were many guilty as charged? Undoubtedly.

Nixon may have prompted Vice President Spiro Agnew to ask in a television speech, "Who are these people who are on your television screens every night? They tell you what to think but were never elected to anything." In 90 days Mr. Agnew was driven out of office by the media. A few of the same talking heads, or their descendants, are still there every night.

Many people felt, and Nixon was undoubtedly among them, that the Vietnam War was lost in the streets of America aided and abetted by a media that was cozy with the demonstrators, who were duped by the communists in the universities. There is little doubt that the media brought down two Presidents, and a Vice President over the war.

Nixon sat in the room when the whistle was blown by Whittaker Chambers on Alger Hiss and others in the State Department for passing secrets to Russia. He was in Congress when career State Department employees advised our President that Chiang-Kai-Shek was the real enemy of China and deserved to be overthrown. The result was Secretary of State George C. Marshall withdrew all aid from Chiang and China fell to the communists. This pattern was to repeat itself when Fidel Castro was called an agrarian reformer, and Cuba fell to communism.

Remember the campaign to impeach Earl Warren? Nixon was in Washington when the chief justice freed a dozen or so Harvard professors, fired, arrested and convicted, for being card-carrying members of the communist party, and for teaching and advocating the violent overthrow of the United States. They were turned in by other communists who were offered a lighter sentence by turning state's evidence.

Warren freed the prisoners because they had not actually used guns, and he ordered them re-instated in their jobs with freedom to pursue what they had been doing. Reportedly the whistle blowers served their 15-year negotiated sentences.

This effectively changed the laws of treason and allowed Presidential candidate for President George McGovern and actress Jane Fonda (who reportedly cheered when an American plane was shot down within her view, for which she later apologized) to freely travel to North Vietnam and meet with Ho Chi Minh in Hanoi, thus encouraging an enemy actively engaged in killing other Americans.

It allowed college students to riot in the streets, chanting, "Go,go, Ho Chi Minh" ostensibly against the war, but effectively in support of an enemy that was killing American soldiers.

There was a feeling among military people and probably by Nixon during this period that every student alienated from his government by the riots was a casualty of the war as surely as if he or she had been shot or captured by the enemy.

Hardly ever reported in the media, but well known in intelligence circles, was the 20-year communist plan for world conquest issued in the early 1950s. It outlined how they would over-run Europe, Africa and the masses of Asia, and how by about 1973, the U.S. would fall into their hands like ripe plum.

It did not go un-noticed in anti-communist circles that in 1973, a candidate for President of the United States, who had participated in street demonstrations in support of the enemy, had boldly visited the communist enemy in his own capital while Americans were being killed. In any other time in America, this would have been an act of treason. This presidential candidate had all the appearance of the ultimate communist mole, and the threat that we were about to fall into communist hands had a real possibility of coming to pass.

Use your head now. Doesn't it seem likely that knowing what he knew, President Nixon would consider it his duty to find out if there were communist connections and if the Soviet Union was behind this candidacy?

When chief of staff, H. R. Haldeman, was testifying before the Watergate committee, I was sitting on the edge of my chair in front of the television expecting to hear why the President thought the Watergate break-in was necessary, and what they had discovered.

Mr Haldeman started to answer, "First, you must understand the tenor of the times…" He was cut off in mid-sentence and was never allowed, nor was anyone else allowed, to pursue this defense. "Did you, or did you not," was the tenor of the times.

If Nixon had insecurities they probably were more for the future of his country than personal.

136

APPENDIX D

Proposed Plan of Action for Defense Against Terrorism in America

Proposed War Time Iimmigration Act For the Period of the War Plus 12 Months

Situation

Beginning in the early 1940s, laws which permitted communism to bring its revolution to American soil without regard to national defense have removed just about every legal action the government had to defend itself. Legal scholars have stated that under present law it would be virtually impossible for America to defend herself against an internal enemy determined to bring her down.

Millions of illegal aliens from the Middle East and elsewhere, have invaded America in the past ten years, whose plans are unknown. Many show a remarkable acquiescence to what the terrorists are doing by refusing to join the war against Terrorism or pledging allegiance to America, and/or they have moved freely into underground cells or sensitive positions that threaten economic destruction of U.S. electronic, military or medical infrastructure.

Attempts to prosecute these acts have been largely ineffective. Americans caught in enemy camps bearing arms against other Americans have been defended under civil law and are getting off with small penalties for acts that in pre-WWII days would have brought a life or even death sentence. Underground activity seems to hold no penalty at all.

Action

Action should be taken under the President's War Powers to return these laws to Pre-WWII status for the duration of the War on Terrorism, plus the time necessary to prosecute sedition.

Message to such aliens:

1. You are required to show up at the county courthouse (on a specified date) with required immigration paperwork that shows your right to be here legally. If your papers pass muster, you will receive an ID card indicating you are eligible to apply for entry into the U.S. and for application for citizenship.

2. Lacking such papers, you will be scheduled for a series of polygraph tests as to your purpose for being here, present or past membership in organizations which are considered un-American, un-willingness to pledge allegiance to America in case of enemy attack, etc. Passing such tests will qualify you to apply for immigration status as in paragraph 1 above. After a period of time, application for citizenship may be considered.

3. Failing to pass the polygraph tests will schedule you for a background check, which if passed, will qualify you to apply for immigration status as in paragraph 1.

4. Failure to pass any of the tests above will subject you to being returned to your country of origin or to such other country as will take you in.

5. Failure to qualify for such return or acceptance by another country, you may be placed in a security camp for the period of the War plus six months, then tested as in paragraph 1 and following.

Un-American Activity

Non-aliens who are in America legally but declare or demonstrate their disloyalty to this country by failure to declare allegiance, giving aid and comfort to an enemy, sabotage, spying, rioting or other activity, or harboring such non-aliens by action, which will do harm to America or its citizens under sedition laws in effect before the start of WWII, will be prosecuted to the limit of the law.

Declared love for America will not substitute for action under this statute. No matter what you say, if you don't love America enough to pledge allegiance to her in preference to all others, then you don't love her enough.

Action to thwart the intent of this law shall be declared Un-American Activity.

Security Zones

Security zones or reservations cut off from the rest of America, will be constructed for the safekeeping of declared enemies, until the War on Terror is over. REW

Note: This is a proposed plan of action by a citizen and is **not** a U. S. Government program.

BIBLIOGRAPHY

Books

Harry Rimmer, *The Coming War and the Rise of Russia,* Wm.B. Eerdman's Publishing Company, 1945.

Harry and Banora Overstreet, *What We must Know About Communism,* Pocket Books, Inc., 1960.

Paul K. Conkin and David Bruner, *A History of Recent America*, Thomas Y. Crowell Company, 1974.

J. Edgar Hoover, *Masters of Deceit,* Pocket Books, Inc., 1960.

W. Cleon Skousen, *The Naked Communist,* The Ensign Publishing Company, 1960.

Thomas W. Pauken, *The Thirty Years War: The Politics of the Sixties Generation*, Jameson Books, 1994.

Ann Coulter, *Treason,* Crown Forum, 2003, New York, NY

Laura Ingraham, *Shut Up and Sing,* Regnery Publishing, Inc., Washington, DC

L. Brent Bozell., *The Warren Revolution,* Arlington House, New Rochelle, NY

Sean Hannity, *Let Freedom Ring,* Regan Books, New York, NY

Mona Charen, *Useful Idiots*, Regnery Publishing Inc., Washington DC

David Brock, *The Seduction of Hillary Rodham,* Simon and Schuster, NY

Gordon Lonsdale, *Twenty Years in Soviet Secret Service*, Hawthorn Books, Inc., New York, NY

Henry Steel Commager, *The American Mind,* Yale University Press, New Haven, CT

George Bush, *All the Best,* Simon and Schuster, New York, NY

George F. Will, *Suddenly*, The Free Press, NY

Publications

William Murchison, "We Are Still Fighting the 30-Year War," *The Dallas Morning News*, March 15,1995.

Los Angeles Times, *The Dallas Morning News,* "Bennett Blasts Hollywood Lyrics, Music," June 8, 1995

David Broder, "FBI Has the Tools to Fight Terrorism," *The Dallas Morning News*, May 3, 1995.

Jim Hoagland,, "Words Can't Obscure Responsibility," *The Dallas Morning News*, April 18, 1995.

Ed Bark, "Vietnam on the Big Screen," *The Dallas Morning News*, April 23, 1995.

Jacquelynn Floyd, "Echoes of Viet Nam," *The Dallas Morning News*, April 23, 1995.

William Murchison, "McNamara Assured Our Defeat," *The Dallas Morning News*, April 19, 1995.

Tim Lee, "McNamara Should Have Stayed at Ford," *The Dallas Morning News*, May 1, 1995.

Associated Press, "American Communists Spying Cited," *The Dallas Morning News*, May 1, 1995.

Ed Timms, "No More War," *The Dallas Morning News*, April 23, 1995.

Austin Bay, "World Remains Too Dangerous Not to Study War," *The Dallas Morning News*, December 30, 1994.

Kate Seago, "Interview With Pete Seeger," *The Dallas Morning News*, January 14, 1996.

Walter Goodman, "Cable Channels Take Us Back to Blacklist Days," *The Dallas Morning News*, February 25, 1996.

John Leo, "Time Warner Is Feeling The Pressure," *The Dallas Morning News,* June 16, 1995.

Lee Hockstader, "Yeltsin Turns His Back On Reform," *The Washington Post*, January 15- February 4, 1996.

Georgie Ann Geyer, "First Amendment is No Defense For Junk TV," *The Dallas Morning News*, March 22, 1996.

Steve Mills. "America's Left Is In Disarray But Not Out Of the Picture," *The Dallas Morning News*, January 13, 1995.

INDEX

143

OTHER WRITING

Robert E. Williams

NEWS
Business and sailing sports writer
and free-lance photo-journalist over 18 years.
Estimated 2,000 published items, features, news,
and photographs in newspapers, magazines and news letters

BOOKS
The Station Keepers
A Naval Aviation History
2000

The Station Keepers
A Naval Aviation History
Second Edition Revised Expanded
2002

EDITOR
The Athenian
Official Newspaper of Athens High School, Athens, Texas
Reproductions of Four Years of
Athens High School Student Newspapers
Classes of 1941, 1942, 1943, 1945
Published especially for the April 4, 1992 Reunion
Certified and Sealed Limited Edition
With Special Discoveries from the
Athens Daily Review
During the War Years
Robert W. Strain Publisher

ABOUT THE AUTHOR

Robert E. "Bob" Williams is a native of Corsicana, Texas. He joined the Army Air Corps in 1942 and became an instrument flying instructor. When the Big War was over, he joined the Naval Air Station Dallas Station Keepers to train pilots and aircrewmen, and in time retired from the Navy. He earned BBA and MBA degrees from Southern Methodist University in evening classes, and was employed in top training and human resources positions by two large corporations until retirement, then owned a sailboat dealership.

Retiring again, he now writes free-lance in multiple venues, and with his wife, Peggy, travels the country in their motor home. His experience as Commodore of the Chandlers Landing Yacht Club led to his being chosen to contribute to the success of the XXVI Sailing Olympics in Savannah, Georgia, in 1996.

He admits to shedding tears at flag ceremonies, and he objects to court decisions that neglect national defense. He joins Thomas Sowell in warning that our "living" Constitution, which changes with the times, is indeed dying and being re-interpreted out of existence, with no consideration for defense against enemies from within.

Bob lives with his wife in Rockwall, Texas. He has two children, six grandchildren and eight great grandchildren.

ENDNOTES

[1] Harry and Bonaro Overstreet: "What we Must Know about Communism," pg

[2] W. Cleon Skousen, *The Naked Communist,* pg 37

[3] J. Edgar Hoover, *Masters of Deceit,* pg 19

[4] Overstreet. op. cit. pg 3-7.

[5] Skousen op. cit. pgs 110-117

[6] Hoover, op. cit pg

[7] Overstreet. op. cit. pg 7-12

[8] Hoover, op. cit pgs 93-97 FXF

[9] Skousen, op., cit 210-213

[10] Thomas W. Pauken, *Thirty Years of War: The Politics of the Sixties Generation*, 78

[11] See Chapter 4, *Brainwashing - A Practical Exercise in Living Under Communism*

[12] Pauken, op. cit. Pg 84

[13] W. Cleon Skousen, *The Naked Communist*, pg 210

[14] Hoover, op. cit pgs 93-97

[15] Michael Medved, *Hollywood vs America*, pg 90

[16] John Leo, "Gutter Talk, TV guiding our disregard *of* civility," Universal Press Syndicate, *The Dallas Morning News*. April 17, 1996

[17] See Appendix A - "Crisis Averted at Berkeley"

[18] Leo, op. Cit.

[19] Conkin and Burner, op. cit., pg 520

[20] Cleon Skousen, *The Naked Communist*, pg 169

[21] *Skousen, Op. cit, Pg 170*

[22] Skousen, op. cit. Pg 185

[23] Skousen, op. cit. Pg 189

[24] Skousen, op. cit. Pg 190

[25] Skousen, op. cit. Pg 192

[26] Skousen, op. cit. pg 194

[27] Skousen, op. cit. pg 194, 195

[28] Skousen, op., cit. pg 195; Pauken, op. cit. pg 37

[29.] Pauken, op.cit. Pg 58

[30] Stanley Rothman & Robert Lichter, "The Roots of Radicalism" as reported by Pauken, op. cit. pg59

[31] Pauken, op. cit. pg 59

[32] Conkin and Burner, op. cit., pg 494

[33] Conkin and Burner, op. cit., pgs 499-501

[34] Skousen, op. cit. pg 144

[35] Steve Mills, *Chicago Tribune*, as published in The Dallas Morning News, January 3, 1995

[36] *The Economist,* "Russia's awful choice" and "A dreadful prospect," March 16-22 1996, pgs 18, 19, 53, 54.

[37] Sowell, op.cit. as reported by Pauken, op.cit. pg 195

[38] *The Dallas Morning News,* April 8. 1995

[39] William Murchison. "We Are Still Fighting The 30-year War," *The Dallas Morning News,* March 15, 1995

[40] Pauken, op. cit. pg 63

[41] Pauken. op. cit. pg 30

[42] Pauken. op. cit. pg 27

[43] As reported in *Harry and Bonaro Overstreet,* "What We Must Know About Communism," pg 193

[44] Overstreet, op. cit., pgs 199-201

[45] Overstreet, op. cit., pgs 205-206

[46] First author unknown.

Printed in the United States
30309LVS00001B/394-441